© Macdonald & Co. (Publishers) Ltd., 1966

First Published in 1966
Second Edition 1968
Third Edition 1970
Macdonald & Co. (Publishers) Ltd.
St. Giles House, 49/50 Poland Street, London, W.1.
Made and Printed in Great Britain by
Waterlow & Sons Ltd., London and Dunstable

NAVIES OF THE

SECOND

WORLD WAR

GERMAN SURFACE WARSHIPS

H. T. LENTON

MACDONALD : LONDON

INTRODUCTION

The Second World War started five years too early for the German Navy. They had planned to build up a balanced navy which, by 1944, would be strong enough to challenge the Royal Navy's command of the seas, but not by outright conflict. It was to be a corsair navy, composed of strong surface groups and a powerful submarine arm, with which depredations on British trade could be made on an unprecedented scale. Fortunately, the plan never materialised, nor was it certain of success, but the challenge would have been a strong one with the issue contested to the bitter end.

Maritime trade was the lifeblood of the dispersed British Empire and its Dominions, and it was both the strength, and weakness, of the British position. With her sea communications secure Great Britain could resist aggression, and wage war all round the world using the ocean highways as a flexible and economic means of transport, and war is principally this matter. But the trade routes were long and vulnerable and none realised this better than the British themselves—and her potential enemies. Despite, one may say in spite of, successive British Governments pre-occupied with disarmament and appeasement, the semblance of a large and powerful fleet was retained, but it was not necessary to probe too deeply to uncover weaknesses and shortcomings in essential categories.

By a vigorous programme spread over ten years (1935–44) the German Navy hoped to cut back their disparity in strength to acceptable limits happily aware that they were not the only navy the British fleet sought to contain. But they suffered two severe setbacks at an early stage: the first was the 1937 British re-armament, and subsequent, programmes; the second was the folly of their leaders in prematurely precipitating a war two years later. The re-armament programme was on a scale not witnessed since pre-1914 which, within the industrial and economic capacity of Great Britain, set out rapidly and drastically to make good the deficiencies in its fleet. It came so late, almost too late, that its impact was never fully appreciated in Germany: they had, in fact, already lost the naval race. German shipbuilding could not keep pace with, much less outstrip, the British capacity, and even had war not intervened there was every indication that German naval construction was under close scrutiny, and that any significant action on their part would result in an immediate, and larger, British counter-action.

From the outbreak of war, therefore, the construction of the German surface ships generally languished, and construction mainly concentrated on submarines. They could dispute but never attain for themselves the command of the seas as they lacked the means to exercise command had they been successful. There is no doubt that sea communications were gravely threatened, but the threat was not basically from the German surface fleet which is listed in this book. It was the nucleus of a fleet that never reached maturity and, as such, was confined to the sidelines. This small fleet conducted itself well in covering the German invasion of Norway but when the ultimate issue presented itself, the invasion of Great Britain, its task was hopeless. There was no way round the stern bulwark presented by the Royal Navy, once more cast in its historic role of defending its native shores. The projected invasion was abandoned. The German Navy achieved some singular and spirited success with their surface ships which, if often spectacular, did not affect the main issues. Meanwhile, its submarine arm relentlessly pursued a *guerre du course* against trade, following a classical but nevertheless false doctrine which has yet to achieve success. The German Navy fought hard, fought long, fought gallantly, but lost. At the outbreak of war their C-in-C was under no illusion of the task ahead and had remarked that "the surface forces . . . are so inferior in number, and strength, to those of the British fleet that . . . they can do no more than show that they know how to die gallantly . . . ." These proved prophetic words.　　　H. T. L.

Battleship TIRPITZ

[*Drüppel*

THE GERMAN NAVY

REBUILDING A FLEET—1919–1939

The Treaty of Versailles dealt a heavy blow to the *Kaiserliche Marine* in 1919. Its best ships—already in custody in British waters—were to be surrendered for division among the victorious Allied powers, while only a token force composed entirely of obsolescent pre-1914 vessels was to be retained to preserve a precarious status quo in the Baltic.

This force was sufficient to ensure that in the chaotic conditions following the 1917 Russian revolution, and subsequent counter-revolution, that Germany was not left entirely defenceless but had some means of resistance at her disposal: and the threat was clearly recognised as coming from the east. Oddly, such military forces that Germany was allowed to retain were to act as an initial bulwark against any proposed, or probable, Bolshevik onslaught, and were not determined by any higher motives. Regardless of whether the negotiations conducted at Versailles were successful, or not, there can be little doubt that the permitted strength of the German Navy allowed by this treaty was finely calculated, and comprised:—

    (a) the battleships *Braunschweig, Elsass, Hannover, Hessen, Lothringen, Preussen, Schlesien,* and *Schleswig-Holstein*

    (b) the light cruisers *Amazone, Arcona, Berlin, Hamburg, Medusa, Niobe, Nymphe,* and *Thetis*

    (c) the destroyers T.175, T.185, T.190, T.196, V.1, V.2, V.3, V.5, V.6, G.7, G.8, G.10, G.11, S.18, S.19, and S.23

    (d) the torpedo boats T.135, T.139, T.141, T.143, T.144, T.146, T.148, T.149, T.151, T.152, T.153, T.154, T.156, T.157, T.158, and T.168,
        and

    (e) ancillary vessels such as minesweepers, surveying vessels, etc.

The active strength was limited to six battleships, six light cruisers, twelve destroyers, and twelve torpedo boats, and vessels in excess of this number were to be held in reserve. No submarines or aircraft were allowed to be kept or built. With personnel restricted to 15,000, the German Navy experienced considerable difficulty in keeping even this small force fully manned, and the active fleet did not, in practice, ever attain its full allotted strength. Replacement tonnage was allowed in all categories, once vessels became over-age, subject to the following limitations: battleships 10,000 tons, light cruisers 6,000 tons, destroyers 600 tons, and torpedo boats 200 tons. If the treaty makers at Versailles showed good judgement on the material side, they failed lamentably on the psychological side if they imagined, by these tonnage limitations, that the German Navy would simply replace old vessels of limited fighting value by only slightly superior new construction. If a single trait was outstandingly obvious with the German race it was their ability, and capacity, for detailed planning—especially in the field of military science. Viewed in this light the Versailles Treaty was a challenge in which every artifice was used by the German armed forces to circumvent the restrictive clauses of the treaty: first by guile and falsehood, and then later by open defiance.

In 1922 a new light cruiser, the *Emden*, was proposed whose design was little advanced on that of the "Dresden" class, the final First World War design to be built. The original provision was to have eight guns twin-mounted on the centre line, but as these mountings failed to materialise she received eight single mountings instead, arranged four on the centre line and four on the broadside. Two years later the first six replacement destroyers, allocated the hull numbers W.102–106, were projected. Ostensibly of 600 tons (they later proved to be over 900 tons—see *Note* [1]) they were not outstanding craft, and followed the traditional German line of flotilla craft with the torpedo armament predominating.

The programmes for 1925 and 1926 embraced three light cruisers, six further destroyers, and a torpedo boat. The light cruisers were of 6,000 tons (6,650 tons), and with a main armament of nine 5.9-inch guns introduced triple mountings to the German Navy. The turrets were disposed one forward and two aft, and the after turrets were arranged *en echelon* to widen their bow arcs and supplement ahead fire. The original provision for four single A.A. guns was increased to six, all twin-mounted, while building, and the torpedo armament of twelve deck tubes was the heaviest fitted to contemporary, or subsequent, foreign cruisers. Not in keeping with the usual German practice was the meagre scale of protection comprising a narrow waterline belt with thin plating to decks and turrets, and was most probably the result of tonnage restrictions which, with these vessels, was not greatly exceeded. The machinery installation consisted of geared turbines and 10-cylinder diesel engines coupled to twin shafts

---

Note [1]: Hereafter, the actual displacement in parentheses will follow the officially stated figures given prior to the outbreak of the Second World War.

and this arrangement was one of the earliest examples of separate prime movers for full speed and cruising purposes.

The torpedo boat, hull number W.108, was not finally proceeded with as the 200-ton restriction proved too severe to enable a useful type of craft to be developed, but the destroyers, hull numbers W.109–114, were generally similar to the earlier type with the addition of some 15 feet in length, while two units carried guns of heavier calibre.

In 1928 work started on a further light cruiser, the *Leipzig*, which adopted a three-shaft machinery arrangement but was otherwise similar to the "K" class above. The geared turbines were coupled to the wing shafts, and four 7-cylinder diesel engines to the centre shaft for cruising purposes. The variable pitch propeller on the centre shaft feathered when the turbines only were used while conversely, when cruising solely on the diesel engines, the wing shafts were spun by B.H.P. 500 motors. The following year's programme included the first battleship replacement, a combined gunnery training and mine-laying vessel, two fishery protection vessels, and the first series of motor minesweepers.

It is here relevant to broadly recall the term of the Washington Naval Treaty which limited capital ships to 35,000 tons and 16-inch guns, and cruisers to 10,000 tons and 8-inch guns. Between them there existed a virtually forbidden zone into which only aircraft carriers encroached, with their upper limit initially placed at 27,000 tons and their ordnance restricted to 8-inch guns. When the treaty was framed particular concern had been expressed that an intermediate class—approximating the old armoured cruiser—may result between capital ships and cruisers which would completely outclass the latter, and resulted in two safeguards being incorporated: a total tonnage limitation on capital ships, and the 8-inch gun restriction on aircraft carriers which were precisely defined as "decked vessels primarily designed to operate aircraft" (see *Note* [2]). This effectively prevented vessels exceeding the cruiser limits being built, as they would then rank as capital ships and be included in the total tonnage for that class, and none of the signatories to the treaty (see *Note* [3]) had any margin to spare in that

---

Note [2]: This resulted in the large British cruisers *Courageous* and *Glorious*, armed with 15-inch guns, either being included in the total tonnage for capital ships or being scrapped. Their retention was secured, however, by converting them to aircraft carriers.

Note [3]: France, Italy, Japan, United Kingdom, and United States of America.

7

category. Similarly, the Treaty of Versailles had restricted German replacement battleship tonnage to 10,000 tons and 11-inch guns, and while apparently keeping within these limits, the German Navy announced details of the first ship they proposed to build to these limitations.

She was to be of 10,000 tons (11,700 tons), 26 knots speed, and primarily armed with six 11-inch guns. With the exception of eight battlecruisers then extant (four British and four Japanese) she justified the claim that she could outfight any vessel she could not outrun. In fact, the German Navy had utilised replacement battleship tonnage to build a vessel which made no pretensions to capital rank, and fell into the forbidden zone the Washington Treaty had so laboured to avoid. For the German naval architects it was a *tour de force* as, compared with her, all foreign cruisers built to the upper limit of the Washington Treaty cut a sorry figure. The pride of nation and navy were fully expressed when she was named *Deutschland*. In the popular press she was hailed as a "pocket battleship", most probably because she was neither one or the other, but in the German Navy she was simply rated *panzerschiff* (armoured ship), which could be liberally translated as armoured cruiser.

Novel features introduced in her construction, for a vessel of her size, were electric welding and main propulsion by diesel engines: both weight saving items, particularly the latter, which gave her a large radius of action on a modest bunkerage, and clearly marked her as a corsair intended to operate against trade. Nor was the impact of the *Deutschland* on the naval sphere lessened by the fact that the German Navy could legally build six such vessels, and intended fully to implement her rights under the treaty.

The *Deutschland* completely overshadowed the remaining vessels included in the programme for the year, and not that they were without interest. The dual purpose *Bremse* was a fast minelayer thinly disguised as a gunnery training ship, and was also largely experimental. She was the test bed for the diesel machinery installed in the *Deutschland*, and also mounted the 5-inch guns later to be fitted to destroyers. The two sloops on the other hand, built for fishery protection duties, were without merit, but the motor minesweepers, R.1–16, were the prototypes of a subsequent large series which performed ubiquitous service comparable to the British Fairmile "B" motor launches. They provided early experience in the construction of small, fast, round bilge form craft, and were equally adaptable for patrol, anti-submarine, or escort work besides their designed role.

The small craft programme was continued in the following year with the first motor torpedo boats, and as a result a significant step was taken a few years later when the German Navy placed a development contract with M.A.N. and Daimler-Benz to produce a suitable lightweight diesel engine for coastal craft. In the interim, hull form was further developed, after extensive tank tests had resulted in the adoption of the round bilge form for seaworthiness, and a high L:B ratio for speed. Alone among the navies of the world the German Navy introduced, and retained, this hull for their M.T.B.'s.; again alone they had the prime advantage of being able to power them with diesel engines; and technically their development and subsequent production was of the highest order.

The programmes for the years 1931 and 1932 each included further armoured ships, the *Admiral Scheer* and *Admiral Graf Spee*, and the following year included a battle cruiser, light cruiser, eight fast sloops, eight submarines, two submarine depot ships, a yacht, and additional M.T.B.'s.

The armoured ships basically followed the *Deutschland* but with modified bridge and superstructure and heavier calibre A.A. guns, increased from 3.5-inch to 4.1-inch. However, the introduction of the *Deutschland* had not passed unchallenged and resulted in the French Navy laying down two 26,000-ton battlecruisers, which not unnaturally completely outclassed her, and there were indications that the French action would be followed by other navies.

In Germany a new leader had emerged: an outspoken militarist determined to regain for Germany her former greatness, and by force where other means failed. He shrewdly recognised that the victors of the First World War now only possessed the illusion of great powers, were unwilling in the military sense to pay the price this role demanded, and that their voices carried less conviction in distinct proportion to their annually declining armed strength. Faced with former allies that no longer acted in concert, and all possessing strong pacifist elements, he used this disunity to full advantage and rallied all Germany behind him. The name of Adolf Hitler has since passed into history, and with his rise to power a cloak of deception fell over German naval activities. There was no point in proceeding with the fourth "Deutschland" as planned—the type had been surpassed—and the vessel was consequently turned into a 26,000-ton (31,800-ton) battlecruiser, the *Scharnhorst*, a fast and robust vessel which sacrificed gunpower, and not protection, for speed. Although submarine construction had been banned design work had been undertaken as outlined in the companion volume (see *Note*[4]) to these books, and eight coastal submarines, U.1–8, and two depot ships were ordered. But these orders were cloaked in

Note [4]: *Navies of the Second World War: German submarines* (Macdonald & Co. Ltd., London. 1965).

secrecy, although the enlarged *Scharnhorst* was suspected. Thus, in little over a decade, the Versailles Treaty was abrogated, but a further two years was to pass before it was officially recognised.

No secret was made about the remaining vessels of the programme. The light cruiser *Nürnberg*, 6,000 tons (6,980 tons), closely followed the *Leipzig* but with the A.A. armament increased to eight 3.5-inch guns, all twin mounted. On 600 tons (712 tons) the sloops were fast and well-armed, but their exact function was obscure as they were too superior for some roles, and inferior for others. For escort, or anti-submarine, work they possessed a large excess of speed, while they were too slow for employment with the torpedo flotillas, and had too restricted a radius to work with the fleet. The German Navy tended to assign dual purpose roles to their minor war vessels in order that they could be fully employed as combatant units in time of war, but the results were sometimes surprising. The yacht *Grille*, officially rated as a sloop, was an expensive luxury but a suitable status symbol for the Head of State. Although possessing a good turn of speed and an adequate radius of action she lacked any military value.

Undisclosed in the 1934 programme was another battlecruiser, the *Gneisenau*, two heavy cruisers sixteen destroyers, and twenty-eight submarines; while two further sloops, another gunnery training ship, and additional M.T.B.'s and M.M.S's. were publicised. The *Gneisenau* was a sister ship to the previous year's *Scharnhorst*, and together they matched the French pair built to counter the "Deutschlands". The heavy cruisers *Admiral Hipper* and *Blücher*, 10,000 tons (13,900 tons) and armed with eight 8-inch guns, and the destroyers Z.1–Z.16, 1,625 tons (2,170/2,270 tons) and armed with five 5-inch guns and eight torpedo tubes, were also in plain defiance to the Versailles Treaty, and taken together with the battlecruisers were the nucleus of a fleet whose horizon was no longer limited by the Baltic and coastal waters.

Filling the dual roles of training ship and minelayer was the *Brummer*. Unlike the *Bremse* she adopted turbine machinery and was considerably slower, but like her she was used experimentally and was fitted with very high pressure boilers that were later installed in cruisers, destroyers, and torpedo boats. In spite of the success they enjoyed in the *Brummer* they were, on the whole, rather a disastrous innovation, which resulted in many boiler failures under the rigours of war steaming with its frequent demands for high, and sustained, steam production. The large mine deck could stow four hundred and fifty mines, and when stripped could otherwise accommodate 450 men for training purposes.

The M.T.B.'s, S.10–13, were similar to the previous year's boats, S.7–9, except that they had Daimler-

Benz instead of M.A.N. diesel engines, but the M.M.S's., R.17–24, were considerably increased in size over the prototypes, with displacement raised to 115 tons from 60 tons, and the installed engine power practically trebled with a corresponding rise in speed. Even though the development project placed with diesel engine manufacturers had not yet borne fruit, there was still no difficulty in obtaining suitable units for installation *pro tem*, and no other navy in the world was so advantageously placed in this respect.

By 1935 there was no longer any doubt that Germany was re-arming on a large scale, although precise details were lacking. Any doubts were soon dispelled when, in an historic statement in the early part of the year, Hitler publicly repudiated the Versailles Treaty, and proclaimed Germany's right to determine her own future. In the total absence of any concerted action by the convening powers at Versailles to check this growth, the British and German governments entered into an agreement whereby the German Navy limited itself to 35 per cent of the Royal Navy in total tonnage. Included in this total figure were submarines, but in this category Germany reserved the right to equality with the Royal Navy, but stated her intention not to exceed 45 per cent without giving further notice. It is interesting to note that limitations were in terms of total tonnage, and not qualitative or quantitative, and any increase in submarine over 35 per cent would, therefore, be balanced by an equal reduction in other categories. This bi-lateral agreement did not meet with universal accord, but the British government was on firm ground whereby they limited German naval re-armament in the absence of any restriction that could be placed on it.

Based on the existing strength of the Royal Navy at that time, and while it was still subject to the Washington and (first) London naval treaties, this agreement allowed the German Navy the following tonnages against the principal categories shown:—

TYPE	TOTAL TONNAGE	BUILT OR BUILDING	BALANCE FOR NEW CONSTRUCTION
Battleships	183,750 tons	82,000 tons	101,750 tons
Heavy cruisers	51,380 tons	20,000 tons	31,380 tons
Light cruisers	67,270 tons	35,600 tons	31,670 tons
Aircraft carriers	47,250 tons		47,250 tons
Destroyers and torpedo boats	52,500 tons	35,600 tons	16,900 tons
Submarines (see *Note* [5])	18,445 tons	12,425 tons	6,020 tons
Totals	420,595 tons	185,625 tons	234,970 tons

From the foregoing it will be seen that the tonnage available for new construction enabled the German Navy, providing they kept within the general qualitative restrictions to which they were not subject, to add the following vessels: three battleships of 35,000 tons each; three heavy cruisers of 10,000 tons each; three light cruisers of 8,000 tons each; two aircraft carriers of 23,000 tons each; six destroyers of 1,625 tons each; twelve torpedo boats of 600 tons each; and eight submarines of 740 tons each.

The overt construction planned before the 1935 agreement could now be revealed, and if added to

Note [5]: The tonnage for submarines using the 45 per cent ratio was 23,715 tons, leaving a balance of 11,290 tons for new construction.

the balance available for new construction outlined above, entailed a large programme of construction which would have to be spread over several years. Not surprisingly the programme for 1935 was a large one, and comprised one battleship, the *Bismarck*, of 35,000 tons (41,700 tons); one heavy cruiser, the *Prinz Eugen*, of 10,000 tons (14,800 tons); one aircraft carrier, the *Graf Zeppelin*, of 19,250 tons (23,200 tons); six destroyers, Z.17–22, each of 1,811 tons (2,411 tons); twelve torpedo boats, T.1–12, each of 600 tons (840 tons); eight submarines, U.37–44, each of 740 tons (1,032 tons); and twelve minesweepers, M.1–12, each of 600 tons (717 tons). There was thus no category in which the standard displacement was not exceeded, and in some cases grossly so. It is, however, fair to add that as none of the first three vessels were completed until after the outbreak of the Second World War, their actual displacements were the result of further increases from this date when, naturally, all restrictions ceased to apply. In this respect the actual breakdown of weights for the *Bismarck* are of considerable interest, and are listed below:—

Hull	11,691	tons	Stores	155½	tons
Armour	17,540	tons	Fresh water (domestic)	167	tons
Main machinery	2,800	tons			
Auxiliary machinery	1,428	tons	*Standard*	42,343½	tons
Armament	5,973	tons			
Aircraft fittings	83	tons	Oil fuel	6,452	tons
Light arms	8	tons	Gas oil	193	tons
Equipment	408	tons	Lub. oil	160	tons
			Petrol	34	tons
Light ship	39,931	tons	Feed water	375	tons
			Reserve feed water	389¼	tons
Ammunition	1,510½	tons			
Small arms ammunition	2½	tons	*Full load*	49,946¾	tons
Complement	243½	tons	Emergency oil fuel	1,009	tons
Provisions	194¼	tons			
Fresh water (drinking)	139¼	tons	*Emergency full load*	50,955¾	tons

The most interesting feature of the *Bismarck* was the extent of her protection, which absorbed more than 40 per cent of her standard displacement, associated with her great beam. Her main belt was 16 feet deep and enclosed the end barbettes, and over this was placed an upper belt which gave her armoured freeboard over the greater part of her length. The upper deck was 3¼ inches thick at its outer edge and thinned to 2 inches amidships, while the lower deck was similarly 4½ inches (sloped) and 3¼ inches (flat) except over the magazines where it was thickened to 4¼ inches and 4 inches respectively. Inboard of the main belt was an armoured longitudinal bulkhead 1½ inches thick above, and 1¾ inches thick below, the lower deck. The turret crowns were angled to increase the obliquity of impact and could consequently be made thinner than the vertical walls. The *Bismarck's* main armament of eight 15-inch guns was not outstanding, but the equal of any afloat, and she adhered to secondary and tertiary batteries, for use against light surface craft and aircraft, whereas American and British contemporaries were more economically minded with their dual purpose secondary armament.

The *Graf Zeppelin* was the German Navy's first experience with an aircraft carrier, and in this respect they were at a severe disadvantage. Coupled to this was the complete lack of co-operation between the German naval and air forces, and at no stage in the *Graf Zeppelin's* chequered career was her air group ready and available to be embarked. Her A.A. armament was good but not ideally placed, before and abaft the island superstructure, where it could only engage targets to port by firing across the flight deck and impede, if not to wholly arrest, simultaneous flying operations. Eight twin 5.9-inch guns, carried on the broadside in armoured casemates at main deck level, were needless additional weight, and such protection as there was confined to the hull leaving the hangars and flight deck quite unprotected. Her construction was halted in August, 1940, when 80 per cent complete, resumed in 1942 to a modified design, but was finally suspended again in April, 1943.

The *Prinz Eugen* generally followed the lines of the earlier heavy cruisers with a slight all-round increase in dimensions and displacement unaccompanied by any other improvements, and the same applied to the second group of destroyers. The torpedo boats, on the other hand, clearly showed the German propensity for the torpedo and were armed with six deck tubes but only a single gun, mounted right aft. The minesweepers were modern counterparts to those built during the First World War, but this was not a class of vessel in which outstanding advances were to be expected. They could do their job, were seaworthy, and although they reverted to reciprocating machinery this was no retrogade step but a clear recognition of available facilities, both in peace and war.

The programmes for the two following years were extensions to that for 1935, and underlined the difficulties experienced by the German Navy in attaining the total tonnage permitted by the Anglo-German Naval agreement. The shipyards were incapable of the required rate of production, and added to this was the difficulty in providing adequate numbers of trained personnel. Ships proposed in 1936 were the battleships *Tirpitz*, a sister ship to the *Bismarck*; a second aircraft carrier; two 10,000-ton (14,800-ton) cruisers, the *Seydlitz* and *Lützow*, to be armed with twelve 5.9-inch guns; eleven submarines, U.45–55, each of 517 tons (753 tons); and the depot ship *Tanga*; to be followed in 1937 by a third battleship, six torpedo boats, twenty-six submarines, six more minesweepers, and two depot ships.

Also in 1937 the German government signed a further naval agreement with the United Kingdom which, in effect, secured their adherence to the qualitative restrictions of the (second) London Naval Treaty. An additional clause was not to build cruisers exceeding 8,000 tons armed with guns larger than 6-inch calibre, which inferred the abandonment of construction of the *Seydlitz* and *Lützow*. However, these two vessels were only shortly in abeyance as the next year Germany legally exercised her rights, under both agreements, to expand her submarine arm up to parity with the Royal Navy, and not only to complete the two cruisers but to arm them with 8-inch guns. Her reasons were based on reports of Russian cruiser and submarine construction to which she felt compelled to reply, although the more reasonable counter to submarines appeared at the time to be anti-submarine vessels and not craft of the same type.

In retrospect, the years 1937/8 were of more than passing interest. They saw the beginning of the British naval re-armament programme whose implications were not fully realised at the time: especially in Germany where the inevitability of war with the United Kingdom was recognised, but not until about 1944/5. The German Navy accordingly drew up plans for the fleet required for this purpose in order to wage war principally against trade on, below, and above the seas, and the estimates were for:—

Six battleships to be completed by 1944,

Four heavy cruisers by 1943, and four more by 1945,

Four light cruisers by 1944, and thirteen more by 1948,

Two aircraft carriers by 1941, and two more by 1947, and

One hundred and twenty-eight submarines by 1943, and ninety-five more by 1947.

To this could be added the existing fleet of two battleships (both building), two battlecruisers, three armoured cruisers, three heavy and five light cruisers (*Emden* was excepted), and forty-four submarines. The plan was modified, from time to time, to suit tactical re-assessment and building capacity, and at least two (if not all) the heavy cruisers were dropped and three battlecruisers added. As was stated earlier, there was no denying the German ability for detailed military planning: but where they failed was to distinguished between actual and proposed. Of the proposed additions only one battleship, two aircraft carriers, and two heavy cruisers had been ordered by the German Navy, and the remainder were still paper projects in 1937 and a long way from fulfilment. At the same time the Royal Navy possessed a present overwhelming superiority in all categories, and the fact to be considered, once the extent of the German programme was known, was to what extent would the United Kingdom retaliate. The answer was to be found in the British estimates for 1937 which were on a higher ratio than ship-for-ship. The German plan could have succeeded only if the subsequent British estimates up to 1941—as ships laid down during these years would have been available by 1944/5—had been nil: an improbability which hardly merited consideration. The British estimates had already shown their awareness of the increased tempo in warship building, and in a building race Germany could not match, far less surpass, the United Kingdom capacity. The German threat was very real in that the Royal Navy could not concentrate the entire fleet in Home waters, in view of heavy commitments in both the Far East and the Mediterranean, but nor did the Royal Navy contemplate having to wage war simultaneously in all three theatres completely unaided.

With the build-up of tension the 1938 programme was not unnaturally a heavy one, and comprised two battleships, two light cruisers, six destroyers, three torpedo boats, thirty-five submarines, six minesweepers, two depot ships, and two icebreakers, plus a variety of smaller craft.

The two battleships, together with the one ordered in the preceding year, were armed as the *Bismarck* and *Tirpitz* except that the main guns were increased to 16-inch calibre, but size rose sharply to 56,200 tons for a dimensionally larger hull. Protection was on the same generous scale as the smaller battleships but sub-division was enhanced by a further increase of beam to 123¼ feet. To secure a large radius of action main propulsion was by twelve 9-cylinder diesel engines coupled to three shafts and totalled B.H.P. 165,000—the most powerful diesel installation ever envisaged.

The light cruisers kept within the limits of the Anglo-German agreements, and were vessels of 7,800 tons, with a main armament of eight 5.9-inch guns, disposed in four turrets, and stowage for 160 mines. They were only lightly armoured, as the *Nürnberg*, with the main deck made a little thicker, and adopted a similar machinery layout, geared turbines coupled to wing shafts and four 12-cylinder diesel engines to the centre shaft, but with power much increased for a top speed of 35½ knots. The destroyers, Z.23–28, were a further increase on size to accommodate the heavier gun armament which had increased to 5.9-inch in calibre: the two forward guns being housed in a twin turret. There was no change in the design of the torpedo boats, T.19–21, or in the six minesweepers, M.19–24, which were continuations of earlier series. The two depot ships and two icebreakers indicated the need for other than pure fighting ships in the balanced build-up of a fleet, and the former were supplemented by four mercantile conversions.

In the field of smaller craft the diesel engine development project placed in 1934 had borne fruit and resulted in the final adoption of a 20-cylinder Daimler-Benz V-form unit—which was to give sterling service in the ensuing years—in preference to the M.A.N. in-line engine. The new engine was first fitted to the M.T.Bs. S.18–25 and proved superior to he alternative unit fitted in the M.T.B's. S.14–17. Production was standardised around these boats, which were otherwise identical and had given every satisfaction in service. However, if the Daimler-Benz engine was more suited to the M.T.B's., the M.A.N. engine was preferred for the lower powered and slower M.M.S's. which shipped them to the exclusion of all else. The smaller series of M.M.S's., FR.1–12, were for river work and were only briefly perpetuated. In spite of being lengthened they were unsuitable for work in open waters, and there was little need to specialise with a purely river craft whose functions, when the need arose, could be undertaken by requisitioning suitable commercial craft, of which there was no shortage.

Also planned in 1938 was a destroyer designed to be mass produced and act as a screen for the raiding squadrons of capital ships, cruisers, and aircraft carriers under construction. They were of more modest dimensions than the heavy units built, or building, and would have probably served the German Navy better than the programme of larger, and more complicated, vessels on which they were embarked, The flush decked design embraced four 5-inch guns in twin turrets fore and aft, eight torpedo tubes in two deck mountings, a wholly adequate speed of 36½ knots, and the exceptional radius of 9,500 miles: on which figures they ranked with comparable vessels anywhere in the world.

In spite of the proposed build-up of the German Navy, the programme for 1939 had to be tailored to suit the available building capacity, and was limited to one battleship, two light cruisers, nine destroyers, three torpedo boats, eleven submarines, three minelayers, six minesweepers, one depot ship (plus two mercantile conversions), a surveying vessel, and further M.M.S's.

The battleship was the fourth 56,200-ton unit, and the light cruisers, destroyers (Z.29–37), submarines, and minesweepers (M.25–30) further additions to earlier classes. The three torpedo boats, T.22–24, were of an enlarged type with the gun armament increased to four 4.1-inch pieces and a reduction in speed of some two knots. The minelayers approached cruiser dimensions and were propelled by geared turbines at 28 knots. They were armed with eight 4.1-inch A.A. guns, twin mounted, except for one unit which shipped four single 5-inch guns and doubled as a gunnery training ship, and could stow up to four hundred mines. Provision was also made for a single aircraft, stowed in a hangar aft, and handled by a crane or otherwise recovered by the Hein mat method, which could be streamed aft through a cut made in the stern. Once again these ships illustrated the lack of precise function which characterised intermediate types of German warships. They were too slow to carry out lays in enemy waters, expensively fast—to the detriment of other qualities—for lays in waters free from enemy interference, and although possessing a good A.A. armament had too restricted a radius to work with the fleet, and were too large and vulnerable to expose as convoy escorts, if employed in an anti-aircraft role in both instances.

The diesel-engined surveying vessel had a quite exceptional radius sufficient to circumnavigate the world, but was also designed with a military view in mind, and was both fast and well armed to fill a detached marauding role against trade. The M.M.S's., R.41 up, were a little larger than, but otherwise similar to, the preceding series, while the smaller type, MR.1–10, similarly increased in size, were the final effort in this direction after which further development with these craft was abandoned.

Thus, in spite of intensive building up to the outbreak of the Second World War, which descended precipitately on the German Navy, the fleet was no match for the Anglo-French combination with which it was now confronted. For the German Navy it was a time of painful re-appraisal to meet a new and unexpected turn of events. There was now no question of challenging the command of the seas, only a war against trade to conduct, but without the backing of a main fleet—the sole means by which command, once gained, was exercised. Force of circumstances had committed the German Navy to a *guerre du course*: a popular but false doctrine yet to be justified.

Although it was originally intended to proceed with the construction of the major units outlined in the 1936/9 programmes, the German Navy, in committing itself to a mainly trade war, soon found that submarine construction was awarded the highest priority, and that all plans for a balanced fleet had to be abandoned.

Limited numbers of destroyers, torpedo boats, etc., were built during the war years, but the major constructive effort among surface vessels was in motor torpedo boats, and fleet and motor minesweepers. For the mining, minesweeping, and the safe passage of convoys along a coastline stretching from the North Cape to the French Biscay ports, a considerable force of auxiliary vessels was put into service, which were essentially dependant on land-based air power for support. Therefore, with the exception of some sporadic forays by small groups of, or individual, ships, surface operations were largely restricted to that within the radius of shore-based aircraft, and vitally dependent on their availability. These conditions did not apply in the Baltic and, to a lesser extent, the Black seas where, in the face of weak opposition, the German Navy was able to secure local command.

War alterations followed a similar pattern experienced by other combatant navies. Firstly, the A.A. armament was augmented by the simple addition of several light pieces—usually single 20 mm.—and sea and air warning RDF was added. Next, the light A.A. armament was further augmented by the addition of multiple 20 mm. and single and twin 37 mm. mountings, which entailed the removal of some original items of equipment to compensate for the increased topweight, and more sophisticated warning and gunnery control RDF was added. This latter enabled aircraft, where carried, to be landed as although RDF did not possess the range of reconnaissance aircraft it gave ample warning, which could be extended depending on the number of vessels operating together, and resulted in a welcome reduction in topweight.

In summarising war construction it is more convenient to work right through each category of ship, as to arrange the sequence of events chronologically would break continuity, and entail considerable repetition in the absence of precise details of the annual war programmes which were recast several times in the course of a single year.

BATTLESHIPS: Two further units of 56,200 tons were projected bringing the total of this class to six. Of these, only the first two were ever laid down, no work took place on the remainder, and all were cancelled in 1940. The following design studies were undertaken during the war, but they were never more than interesting paper projects which illustrate the dimensions to which the German Navy was prepared to expand to secure invulnerability for ships of capital rank. The *H.41* design was for a battleship of 64,000 tons, but this was soon abandoned for the undermentioned successive, and more ambitious, projects:—

H.42 design: 83,265 tons (90,000 tons full): $1001\frac{1}{4} \times 140\frac{1}{2} \times 38\frac{3}{4}$ ($62\frac{3}{4}$d.) feet: belt 15 inches; deck 13 inches; geared turbines (outer shafts) and diesel motors (inner shafts) S.H.P. 160,000 + B.H.P. 120,000 = $32\frac{1}{4}$ knots.

H.43 design: 103,342 tons (111,000 tons full): $1083\frac{1}{4} \times 140\frac{1}{2} \times 39\frac{1}{4}$ (66d.) feet: geared turbines (inner shafts) and diesel motors (outer shafts) S.H.P. 160,000 + B.H.P. 120,000 = 31 knots: eight 19.7-inch (4 × 2) guns.

H.44 design: 122,000 tons (141,500 tons full): $1132\frac{1}{4} \times 169 \times 41\frac{1}{2}$ (69d.) feet: geared turbines (inner shafts) and diesel motors (outer shafts) S.H.P. 160,000 + B.H.P. 120,000 = 30 knots: eight 20-inch (4 × 2) guns.

BATTLECRUISERS: Three units were projected but no constructional work was undertaken on them, and they, too, were cancelled in 1940. The overriding requirement was for speed and radius, and armament and protection was sacrificed to this end. Main propulsion was by four 24-cylinder V-form diesel engines coupled to each wing shaft, for sustained high speed cruising, boosted by geared turbines coupled to the centre shaft to attain the designed full speed of $33\frac{1}{2}$ knots. On a larger scale they were a reversion to the principle adopted by the *Deutschland* of outrunning whatever they could not outfight, and there is no doubt that their destruction could only have been accomplished by (*a*) the heavy gunfire of capital ships providing they could be brought to action, or by (*b*) torpedoes from fast surface vessels and/or aircraft. Their armament was limited to six 15-inch guns in twin turrets, two forward and one aft, and to six 5.9-inch and eight 4.1-inch A.A. guns, all twin-mounted. These were numerically light batteries but underlined their role, which was more to run than fight, and lure enemy capital ships engaging them towards the heavy support groups formed by the battleships referred to above. Although vertical protection, and that to the main turrets and barbettes, was scaled down, horizontal protection remained on practically the same scale as that given to the *Bismarck* and *Tirpitz*.

It was also intended to re-arm the *Scharnhorst* and *Gneisenau* by replacing their triple 11-inch with twin 15-inch turrets, but this was not proceeded with following the complete abandonment of the capital ship programme. The light A.A. armament of these ships was, however, considerably augmented by the addition of a large number of 20 mm. guns, in quadruple, twin, and single mountings, disposed overall. All combatant navies engaged in the Second World War experienced the same necessity for this modification in all types of vessels.

AIRCRAFT CARRIERS: Principally because of the lack of co-operation between the naval and air forces the progress of these units were not greatly advanced. In conjunction with the battleships and battle-cruisers they were to be used against trade, besides providing air cover and long range reconnaissance for the heavy units. In 1940 the *Graf Zeppelin* was suspended as her heavy A.A. armament had been purloined for use ashore, and it would take another year to manufacture and install a new outfit, in addition to the added difficulties in providing fire control equipment for which there were higher priorities in other categories. The second carrier, only a little advanced on the slips, was cancelled owing to shortages of material and labour, but even at this early stage the conversion of a heavy cruiser, the *Seydlitz*, to a carrier was put in hand. By 1942 the need for carriers to support heavy units operating against convoys bound to, and from, Russia by the northern route was stressed, and work on the *Graf Zeppelin* was resumed and the following mercantile conversions were proposed:—

    Europa (1930) 49,746 tons gross: 890 × 102 × 48d. feet: 4-shaft geared turbines S.H.P. 95,000 = 27½ knots: twelve 4.1-inch A.A. (6 × 2), twenty 37mm. A.A., thirty-six 20mm. A.A. guns, forty-two aircraft, two catapults.

    Gneisenau (1935) 18,160 tons gross: 610 × 74 × 45d. feet: 2-shaft geared turbines S.H.P. 26,000 = 21 knots: eight 4.1-inch A.A. (4 × 2), ten 37mm. A.A., twenty-four 20mm. A.A. guns, twenty-four aircraft, two catapults.

    Potsdam (1935) 17,528 tons gross: 597 × 74 × 45d. feet: 2-shaft turbo-electric S.H.P. 26,000 = 21 knots: eight 4.1-inch A.A. (4 × 2), ten 37mm. A.A., twenty-four 20mm. A.A. guns, twenty-four aircraft, two catapults.

In addition, work was proceeding with decking over the *Seydlitz*, and her armament had been altered to ten 4.1-inch A.A. (5 × 2), eight 37mm. A.A., and twenty-four 20mm. A.A. guns, twenty-four aircraft, and two catapults.

In spite of determined efforts none of the carriers were finally completed and the mercantile conversions not even started, and although better relations existed between the naval and air forces from 1943 it was too late, by then, to offset the critical shortages in material and labour which finally hampered progress.

CRUISERS: The final pair of heavy cruisers, the *Seydlitz* and the *Lützow*, were never completed. The former was selected for conversion to an aircraft carrier (see above), and the latter was sold to the Russian Navy while still under construction, and her name given to the armoured ship *Deutschland*. The ex-*Lützow* was delivered in an incomplete state to the Russians, lacking all fire control equipment, and under cover of a multitude of excuses its delivery was deliberately withheld. Although the machinery was installed, it had never been operated, and after she had been sunk in shallow water by German aircraft she was used as a battery by the Russians. After the end of hostilities, the Russian Navy—having meanwhile acquired the *Seydlitz*—intended refitting both ships, which included replacing the twin 8-inch by triple 7.1-inch turrets, but the work involved was so extensive that the project was finally abandoned.

Two more 7,800-ton light cruisers were ordered, but they—together with the four earlier units—were not proceeded with and cancelled between 1941/3. But to provide some screening force for heavy units already completed, the orders for three type 1936A (Mob) destroyers, Z.40–42, placed in 1940 were cancelled, and replaced in the following year by an equal number of scout cruisers. This was basically a blown-up destroyer design, with the foc's'le deck extended well aft and the main armament of 5.9-inch paired in three turrets, one forward and two aft, and the addition of a twin 3.5-inch A.A. mounting, also placed aft. A three-shaft machinery arrangement was adopted, with geared turbines on the wing shafts and four diesel engines coupled to the centre shaft, and by this means the radius was increased to the wholly adequate figure of 12,000 miles. Quintuple banks for torpedo tubes were first projected with this design, and two mountings were placed amidships on the foc's'le deck between the funnels, while upper deck stowage was provided for one hundred and forty mines, almost double that usually carried by a destroyer. Except for thin plating to the turrets and barbettes, no armour was worked into the design, whose most noticeable feature was the concentration aft of the gun armament, superimposed at three levels on the centre line.

The regular cruisers were supplemented by eleven auxiliary units, converted from suitable fast cargo ships, for use against trade. Between them they sank one hundred and thirty-five ships totalling 830,588 tons gross and one cruiser, the *Sydney*, a most creditable performance, and one which outshone the record of the six regular warships (see *Note* [6]) used against trade who accounted for sixty-two ships of 352,027 tons gross and two auxiliary cruisers, the *Rawalpindi* and *Jervis Bay*.

DESTROYERS: Five more destroyers, Z.38–42, were added to the type 1936A (Mob) making twelve in all: but of these the contracts for the final three were cancelled and replaced by orders for three scout cruisers (see above). The destroyers of this, and the preceding series (type 1936A), carried their two forward 5.9-inch guns in a twin turret, with the exception of Z.28, Z.35, and Z.36. However, as the production of these turrets were subject to delay, a single mounting was placed temporarily forward, and the reduction in weight enabled the light A.A. armament to be augmented forward of the bridge. When the turret was finally made available and shipped, these additional light A.A. guns were resited, much farther aft, in place of "C" gun (at the fore end of the after shelter deck) which was removed. The Z.28 was designed as a flotilla leader and differed in that her four guns were all carried singly, two forward and two aft, and extra accommodation was provided at the fore end of the after shelter for the flotilla staff instead of the fifth gun mounted there in the other vessels of these series. The increase in calibre to 5.9-inch for the gun was not a great success, as it was not accompanied by any sensible increase in beam, and the addition of uncompensated topweight made them poorer seaboats in consequence.

With the Z.35 and Z.36, and three subsequent units, Z.43–45, forming the type 1936B, the 5.9-inch guns were replaced by the lighter 5-inch, all mounted singly, and the entire group benefitted by the reduced topweight. Five later units, Z.46–50, while retaining a similar hull and general arrangements as the type 1936B, adopted a new calibre 5.1-inch gun, housed in three twin turrets placed one forward and two aft, and were classed as type 1936C. Although of limited elevation, this new gun could be used as a dual-purpose weapon, and a high angle director was placed aft so that the vessels of this group could engage aerial targets with controlled fire.

Note [6]: These were the battlecruisers *Scharnhorst* and *Gneisenau*; the armoured ships *Deutschland*, *Admiral Scheer*, and *Admiral Graf Spee*; and the heavy cruiser *Admiral Hipper*.

23

The last destroyers ordered during the war met requirements for operations in Northern waters in conjunction with a much greater radius of action. As the very high pressure boilers used in preceding destroyers had far from provided the economy expected in consumption, coupled with lack of reliability, the problem was resolved, startlingly resolved, by adopting diesel engines for main propulsion—the first time it had been applied to destroyers (see *Note* [7]). Not unnaturally work first proceeded with a prototype, the Z.51, which had a diesel engine coupled to each wing shaft, and four units geared to the centre shaft, while the entire installation totalled over B.H.P. 57,000 for a speed of 36 knots. The radius of 13,500 miles was unmatched by any other war-built destroyer at the time. The dual-purpose 5.1-inch gun, introduced with the type 1936C, was retained, and four were equally disposed fore and aft in single mountings, and the usual eight torpedo tubes provided. This vessel was succeeded by the series Z.52–58, which were larger than the prototype and were, in fact, the largest German destroyers contemplated. Although they retained a three-shaft arrangement, the layout was uniform with four diesel engines coupled to each shaft, and the total output was B.H.P. 76,000 for a speed of $37\frac{1}{2}$ knots. The radius was set even higher, at 16,000 miles. They still adhered to the 5.1-inch gun, twin-mounted in three turrets sited two forward and one aft, but introduced new light calibre A.A. guns comprising three 55mm., grouped around the after funnel, and seven twin 30mm. mountings positioned on the bridge, abreast the fore funnel, and well aft. Two high angle directors forward and aft for the main guns, and the absence of funnel caps gave them a distinctive profile among German destroyers. The final outcome was that none were completed: the Z.51 was the furthest advanced and was bombed while completing, material shortages compelled the early cancellation of Z.52–56, and Z.57 and Z.58 were never more than projected.

TORPEDO BOATS: With the authorisation of the type 1934 destroyers, the earlier destroyers of the "Möwe" and "Wolf" classes were re-classed as torpedo boats, and as has already been noted, the type continued in production. A further twelve type 1939 were ordered, bringing the total to fifteen, and

---

Note [7]: In this respect some claim has been made for the U.S. Navy's diesel-electric destroyer escorts, which anticipated the German destroyers in service. But the German vessels were destroyers in the fullest sense, which the American vessels were not, added to which the latter secured their drive by electric motors. In fact, there is no conflict of claim, and both types of vessels introduced novel main propulsion within their categories.

were followed by fifteen similar fleet units with slightly greater power and improved bunkerage and radius.

The next group of nine vessels, T.52–60, dropped the undulating flush-decked hull for a gently sheered long foc's'le with the break occurring well aft. The 4.1-inch guns were grouped in twin A.A. mountings forward and aft with their high angle director placed on the bridge, and were supplemented by a uniform light A.A. armament of twin 30mm. guns. The final group, T.61–72, were all ordered from Netherlands shipyards and their design ante-dated that of their predecessors. Their construction was retarded on every pretext and no more than three reached German ports for final arming and fitting-out. Close on 2,000 tons, their inclusion among torpedo boats is open to question, and they too adopted the raised foc's'le but with the break now placed amidships, abreast the funnel. Unlike other flotilla craft, with the exception of the types 1935 and 1937 torpedo boats, their boiler rooms were adjacent and resulted in a single trunked funnel and distinctive appearance. The gun armament was heavier and comprised four single 5-inch on low angle mountings: an installation not in keeping with then current practice which required main guns to be at least dual-purpose, if not solely anti-aircraft pieces, in view of the heavy air attacks to which they would be exposed at this stage of the war.

TORPEDO RECOVERY VESSELS: The provision of these craft is not easily appreciated in that they possessed the refinements of a small torpedo boat and must, therefore, have absorbed esselntial building capacity which could have been more profitably utilised. Had they been built pre-war, as non-combatant vessels not subject to restrictions or limitations, with the ulterior view to being empoyed, for example, as coastal anti-submarine vessels, their inception would have been understood even if not wholly approved. They had the silhouette of a small torpedo boat, were defensively armed with only two 20mm. A.A. guns, were propelled at 23½ knots by geared turbines, and seemed an expensive way with which to recover practice torpedoes. Eight were built in Germany, TF.1–8, a further sixteen, TF.9–24, were ordered in the Netherlands, and they were all generally similar. They perhaps best reflect the intensity of the German Navy for torpedo warfare, in which they excelled, with the natural corollary that they devoted more than ordinary effort to training that required such specialised vessels.

SLOOPS: One further class, G.1–24, were ordered which were enlarged developments of the earlier class.

Their power output dropped by 50 per cent by the necessity to adopt reciprocating machinery and low pressure boilers, so that an additional boiler was required, and a proportion of their greater size was so absorbed by less efficient and bulkier, machinery, but did enable them to enhance the armament by pairing the 4.1-inch A.A. guns mounted fore and aft. Only G.1 was laid down but was lost incomplete while building in an air raid, and the construction of the remainder, in German and Netherlands shipyards, was abandoned. Later, a smaller series of multi-purpose vessels, MZ.1–12, were put in hand, and were remarkable for the heavy armament of guns and torpedoes accommodated on a small displacement. They were powered by a single diesel engine of B.H.P. 1,000 for a speed of 14 knots but had a restricted radius, at this speed, of only a 1,000 miles. After the initial unit was completed it was planned to lengthen them by $16\frac{1}{2}$ feet but all subsequent construction was cancelled.

MINESWEEPERS: It was in this category that the largest additions were made to the surface fleet. Another two hundred and thirty were ordered of the type commenced pre-war before construction was switched to a smaller, coal burning design for which two hundred and forty-one contracts were placed. Fifteen of the latter were provided with two torpedo tubes on the fo'c'sle for training purposes. The final series were increased in size but remained coal-burning, and over four hundred were projected. They were also designed to be used as anti-submarine or torpedo recovery vessels as the need arose. Of the over nine hundred additions planned about one hundred each of the first and second series, and about four hundred of the final series, were cancelled.

MINELAYERS: Another five large minelayers were projected but, together with the three units planned pre-war, were all cancelled. It should be noted that all destroyers, torpedo boats, and motor torpedo boats were equipped for minelaying and were often used in this role, so that there was no shortage of fast craft to undertake lays in enemy waters. In addition, increasing use was made of submarines and aircraft for this purpose.

MOTOR TORPEDO BOATS: The construction of these boats had been standardised shortly before the outbreak of war, and construction naturally adhered to an established and proven design to speed production. Modifications subsequently incorporated principally related to increased power output and gun armament. The first order for standard boats finally totalled one hundred and five (S.26–29, 38–53, 62–138, and 159–166), of which three (S.100, 136, and 138) had supercharged engines of greater power which were adopted for the second series of four hundred and forty-six boats (S.139–150, 167–500, and 701–800). Power was further increased in two of the latter series (S.170 and 228) but it was too late, by then, to incorporate this advance in a further series, although it was selected for two experimental projects, for hard chine and armoured boats, neither of which finally materialised.

The first standard boats were armed with two 20mm. A.A. guns, placed singly fore and aft, in addition to the two torpedo tubes and two reloads. The torpedo tubes, placed well forward, were enclosed by a half-height foc's'le deck so that the forward gun, mounted between the tubes, was in a well. This innovation was retained throughout the war and considerably added to the seakeeping qualities of these craft. The gun armament was increased, in S.62 up, by replacing the after 20mm. with a 37mm. A.A. gun; by adding a further 20mm. A.A. gun amidships in S.211 up; while S.701 up shipped a uniform armament of twin 20mm. A.A. in all three positions. Earlier boats were later brought up to a comparable standard by substituting a 37mm. for the after 20mm A.A. gun and the addition of a twin 20mm. mounting.

The only departure from the standard boats was for sixteen slightly smaller units (S.30–37 and 54–61) which were lower powered and slower, and whatever unaccountable idea inspired their construction was thereafter dropped.

All these boats could secure an increase in speed of about 2 knots, when running at speed, by the use of side rudders. This adjusted their trim by the stern to a nearly horizontal running plane and resulted in a smaller slope drag.

Two much smaller classes of M.T.B's., LS.1–20 and KS.201–220, of a size that could be hoisted by larger surface vessels, were put in hand. But the restricted employment of such craft, essentially dependant on good weather, outweighed their merits and they were not further developed. One each was carried in the auxiliary cruisers *Komet* (LS.2), *Kormoran* (LS.3), and *Michel* (LS.4), with the boats in the first two altered to stow mines instead of torpedoes.

MOTOR MINESWEEPERS: Unlike the motor torpedo boats, the dimensions of these craft varied with each succeeding group, but the type was otherwise basically unaltered. The group R.130 up advanced to

Forward 15-inch gun turrets (left) and secondary and tertiary batteries (right) of the battleship TIRPITZ [*Drüpp*

140 tons from the 125 tons of the group R.41 up; dropped to 125 tons for the group R.151 up; then again rose to 140 tons (R.218 up) and 175 tons (R.301 up) for the next two groups, which also had more powerful engines; and finally dropped to 140 tons for the last group, R.401 up. Two 21-inch torpedo tubes were added to the largest group and they were renumbered GR.301–320 and used for patrol work, while the gun armament in all boats was strengthened by the addition of three/six 20mm. A.A. guns.

MOTOR LAUNCHES: Only a small number of these craft were built, and none of them in **German** yards, as patrol and escort work was largely undertaken by the motor minesweepers in addition to their

Torpedo boat
TIGER

Drüppel

specialised role. Twelve 70/80-ton craft were built in Denmark, four much smaller boats in Norway, and forty-nine large units in Italy.

MOTOR MINELAYERS: These were small, hard chine form craft, able to carry four mines. Their limited radius of action was on the low side, even for the short distances involved in the southern North Sea, and they were later fitted with two 18-inch torpedo tubes and reclassed as M.T.B's.

EXPERIMENTAL BOATS: These embraced some interesting designs of hydrofoil craft for patrol, mine-laying, transport, and torpedo duties. The principal advantage of hydrofoils lay not in securing a higher speed for a given power, an advantage they none the less possessed, but in their ability to better maintain speed in adverse conditions. The technical difficulties to be overcome, however, were complex, and were not fully resolved even under the stimulus of war conditions.

TRAWLERS AND M.F.V.'S.: Like the Royal Navy these vessels were principally drawn from the fishing fleets for patrol, anti-submarine, and minesweeping duties. But a small trawler and large M.F.V. programme was also put in hand, and design embraced the best mercantile practice and was largely left in the hands of experienced commercial yards.

FERRIES, LIGHTERS AND TRANSPORTS: The first ferries were built for the projected invasion of the United Kingdom in 1940 and were double-ended pontoon supported motor rafts for the carriage of troops and equipment. The later transport ferries were mainly used in the Mediterranean and Black Seas for running supplies and were flat-bottomed but more seaworthy craft, well armed, and partly armoured with 1-inch plate over the engine room and vitals. Some one hundred and twenty were converted to carry a much heavier armament and act as escorts, as these craft were constantly harrassed by attacks from aircraft and light naval forces. The supply lighters, and their gun versions, were similarly employed but in less exposed waters.

All these craft were built in various shipyards at Ancona, Budapest, Castellammare, Genoa, Leghorn, Linz, Monfalcone, Nicolaev, and Vienna under licence from Deutsche Werft, Hamburg.

MISCELLANEOUS VESSELS: Although further depot ships of the same type as the *Otto Wunsche* were proposed, none were actually built, and the only addition in this category were by two more mercantile conversions. Two icebreakers were built in Sweden and a third in the Netherlands; the latter to replace one of the two vessels projected in 1938 but subsequently cancelled.

EX-ENEMY VESSELS: Quite considerable additions were made from this source following the successive campaigns in Poland in 1939; Norway, Denmark, Belgium, the Netherlands, and France in 1940, and finally Italy in 1943, From Italy were seized vessels which they had themselves secured from France, Greece, and Yugoslavia during 1940/1. In addition, a small number of British warships were captured. These additions less submarines which are dealt with in the companion volumes to these books (see *Note* 4), are summarised below, but it should be noted that not all were put into service with the German Navy:—

Polish Navy: four minesweepers and one old sloop.

Royal Norwegian Navy: two coast defence ships, six destroyers (two incomplete), thirteen old torpedo boats, one large and two small minelayers, and two minesweepers.

Royal Danish Navy: two coast defence ships, eight torpedo boats, three sloops, six minesweepers, two minelayers, and one depot ship.

Royal Belgian Navy: two sloops (one incomplete) and two old torpedo boats.

Royal Netherlands Navy: two coast defence ships, one old cruiser, one destroyer (incomplete), two old torpedo boats, three sloops (all incomplete), three minesweepers, ten M.T.B.'s. (all incomplete), and six M.M.S's. (all incomplete).

French Navy: two destroyers (one incomplete), eleven torpedo boats (six incomplete and three ex-Italian), ten sloops (two incomplete), four corvettes (all incomplete), four large (all incomplete and three small aircraft tenders, one minesweeper, and eight submarine chasers.

Royal Hellenic Navy: one destroyer (ex-Italian).

Royal Yugoslav Navy: two destroyers (both ex-Italian), one old torpedo boat (ex-Italian), one seaplane carrier, five M.T.B.'s. (ex-Italian).

Royal Italian Navy: five destroyers, twenty-nine torpedo boats (fifteen incomplete), twenty-four corvettes (fourteen incomplete), forth-three M.T.B.'s., and eighteen M.A./S.B.'s.

Royal Navy: one M.T.B. and one M.L.

Many of these vessels had been scuttled, or sabotaged, to prevent them falling into German hands, and they thus did not rapidly re-inforce the German Navy as perhaps a mere examination of figures indicated.

AUXILIARY VESSELS: Like most major combatant navies, the German Navy during the war acquired a considerable amount of mercantile tonnage to supplement their regular warships. Space does not permit more than passing reference to them, and vessels taken over were placed in service as armed merchant cruisers, escort vessels, anti-submarine and anti-aircraft vessels, patrol vessels, minelayers, minesweepers, mine destroyers, netlayers, cable vessels, weather ships, experimental vessels, training ships of all kinds, target ships, depot ships, repair ships, accommodation vessels, hospital ships, tankers and supply ships, tugs, tenders, etc.

Battleship SCHLESIEN

[*Drüppel*

NAME	BUILDER	LAUNCHED	FATE
Schlesien	Schichau (Danzig)	28.5.06	Scuttled off Swinemünde 4/5/45 after being mined 3/5/45, salved and towed to Königsberg 1947; scrapped 1949.
Schleswig-Holstein	Germania Werft (Kiel)	17.12.06	Scuttled Gdynia 21/3/45 after being bombed R.A.F, aircraft 18/12/44.

These were the last pre-dreadnought battleships to be built for the German Navy, and originally comprised six units of which one, the *Pommern*, was sunk at the Battle of Jutland. Their appearance was not greatly altered but "between the wars" the two foremost funnels were trunked into a single casing, the four upper deck 5.9-inch guns removed, and four single 3.5-inch A.A. guns added on the after superstructure. By the outbreak of war they had been relegated to training, but were used for bombardment purposes in the Polish campaign. They later reduced to harbour service, had their main deck 5.9-inch guns removed, and the A.A. armament considerably augmented.

Displacement: 12,100 tons (14,900 tons full).
Dimensions: 413½(pp) 419(oa) × 72¾ × 25¼/... feet.
Machinery: Eight Marine (oil-fired) + four Marine (coal-fired for training) boilers (pressure 235 lb.); three shafts; reciprocating (VTE), I.H.P. 17,000 = 18 knots.
Bunkers & Radius O.F. 1,130 tons, coal 436 tons; 5,900 miles at 10 knots.
Protection: Main w.l. belt 4 inches (ends)—9½ inches (amid.), upper belt 8 inches, battery 6¾ inches. Deck 1½–2¾ inches. Turrets 6¾–11¼ inches, barbettes 11¼ inches. C.T. 5½–12 inches (fwd.) and 5½ inches (aft).
Armament: Four 11-inch (2 × 2), ten 5.9-inch (10 × 1), four 3.5-inch A.A. (4 × 1), four 20mm. A.A. (4 × 1) guns.
Complement: 725.
Notes: In 1944 the 5.9-inch and 3.5-inch guns were removed, and the A.A. armament increased to six 4.1-inch (6 × 1), ten 40mm. (10 × 1), twenty-two 20mm. (4 × 4 and 3 × 2) guns.

C

Armoured ship DEUTSCHLAND *as completed with single 3.5-inch A.A. guns and catapult not shipped forward of funnel* [*Drüppel*]

NAME	BUILDER	LAUNCHED	FATE
Deutschland	Deutsche Werke (Kiel)	19.5.31	*Lützow* (1940); scuttled Swinemünde 4/5/45 after being bombed Allied aircraft 16/4/45, salved and towed Königsberg 1947; Russian, and scrapped Leningrad 1948/9.

Armoured ship: DEUTSCHLAND

The Treaty of Versailles, by restricting replacement battleship tonnage to 10,000 tons and 11-inch guns, had thought to ensure that new construction would broadly adhere to the pre-dreadnought design, typefied by the *Schlesien* and *Schleswig-Holstein*. But by adopting diesel propulsion and abandoning thick belt and turret armour sufficient weight was saved for a powerful armament and a good turn of speed. Although exceeding the specified limit the illusion was given that the *Deutschland* did not, and every weight saving expedient was exercised in her construction, such as welding, triple turrets for the main armament, etc. The heavy A.A. armament originally comprised four single 3.5-inch guns, all mounted abaft the funnel, but this was later increased to three twin 4.1-inch mountings wider dispersed. The torpedo tubes were carried in armoured shields on the quarterdeck.

Displacement:	11,700 tons (15,900 tons full).
Dimensions:	593(pp) 616¾(oa) × 68 × 19/23¾ feet.
Machinery:	Two shafts; M.A.N. diesel motors (four per shaft), B.H.P. 56,800 = 26 knots.
Bunkers & Radius	O.F. 2,784 tons; 10,000 miles at 19 knots.
Protection:	Main w.l. belt 3¼ inches + 1½ inches internally. Foc's'le deck ¾ inch, main deck 1¼–1½–3 (over magazines) inches. Turrets ½ (rear)–4 (side)–5½ (face) inches, barbettes 4 inches. C.T. 5½ inches with 2-inch hood. Externally bulged.
Armament:	Six 11-inch (2 × 3), eight 5.9-inch (8 × 1), six 4.1-inch A.A. (3 × 2), eight 37mm. A.A. (4 × 2), ten 20mm. A.A. (10 × 1) guns; eight 21-inch (2 × 4) T.T.; two aircraft and one catapult.
Complement:	1,150.
Notes:	A.A. armament augmented by the addition of twelve 20mm. (1 x 4 & 8 x 1) guns and funnel cap added.

Armoured ship ADMIRAL SCHEER *after alterations*   [*Drüppel*

NAME	BUILDER	LAUNCHED	FATE
Admiral Graf Spee	Naval Dockyard (Wilhelmshaven)	30.6.34	Scuttled off Montevideo 17/12/39 after being damaged by gunfire of R.N. cruisers *Achilles*, *Ajax* and *Exeter* 13/12/39.
Admiral Scheer		1.4.33	Bombed Allied aircraft and capsized Kiel 9/4/45 while in dry dock, and buried when dock was filled in.

Modifications of the *Deutschland* with the bridge work made more compact and extended higher, and the aircraft catapult resited abaft the funnel. Dimensions were little altered except for a 3-foot increase in beam, but the main belt was shorter and thicker, and the bunkerage—and consequently radius—slightly reduced.

Displacement: 12,100 tons (16,200 tons full).

Dimensions: 597 (wl) 616¾(oa) × 71¼ × 19/24 feet.

Machinery: Two shafts; M.A.N. diesel motors (four per shaft), B.H.P. 56,800 = 26 knots.

Bunkers & Radius: O.F. 2,436 tons *Ad. Scheer*, 2,523 tons *Ad. Graf Spee*; 9,000 miles at 19 knots.

Protection: Main w.l. belt 4 inches + 1½ inches internally. Foc's'le deck ¾ inch, main deck ¾–1¼–1½–2¼ (over magazines) inches. Turrets ½ (rear)–5 (side)–5½ (face) inches, barbettes 5 inches. C.T. 5½ inches with 2-inch hood. Externally bulged.

Armament: Six 11-inch (2 × 3), eight 5.9-inch (8 × 1), six 4.1-inch A.A. (3 × 2), eight 37mm. A.A. (4 × 2), ten 20mm. A.A. (10 × 1) guns; eight 21-inch (2 × 4) T.T.; two aircraft and one catapult.

Complement: 1,150.

Notes: Clinker screen added to funnel and light A.A. augmented by addition of twenty-six 20mm. guns–later replaced by twelve 37mm. (6 × 2) guns–in *Admiral Scheer* only.

Armoured ship ADMIRAL GRAF SPEE *in the Kiel Canal*

[*Drüppel*

Battlecruiser SCHARNHORST *as completed before addition of clipper bow*

[*Drüppel*

Battlecruiser GNEISENAU *could be distinguished from her sister vessel* SCHARNHORST *as her mainmast was stepped close abaft the funnel*

[*Drüppel*]

The mainmast of the battlecruiser SCHARNHORST *was stepped further aft and carried platforms for additional searchlights* [*Drüppel*

Battlecruiser SCHARNHORST

[*Drüppel*

NAME	BUILDER	LAUNCHED	FATE
Gneisenau	Deutsche Werke (Kiel)	8.12.36	Bombed R.A.F. aircraft Kiel 26/7/42, repairs suspended and scuttled Gdynia 28/3/45; salved 13/9/51 and scrapped.
Scharnhorst	Naval Dockyard (Wilhelmshaven)	3.10.36	Gunfire of R.N. battleship *Duke of York* and torpedoed cruiser *Jamaica* and destroyers *Musketeer*, *Opportune*, *Scorpion* and *Virago* off North Cape 26/12/43.

Battlecruisers: GNEISENAU and SCHARNHORST

These two vessels gave a new slant to the battlecruiser definition by sacrificing weight of armament instead of protection to secure high speed. The heavy A.A. armament of fourteen guns, coupled with four high angle directors, was unmatched for their time. The aircraft catapults were carried high, and mounted over the hangars placed abaft the funnel. The *Scharnhorst* originally had a vertical stem, but this was later altered to the clipper shape adopted by the *Gneisenau*, and she had her mainmast moved further aft from where it was previously stepped, close abaft the funnel, while *Gneisenau* retained this arrangement.

In 1942, while undergoing repairs, the *Gneisenau* was to be lengthened forward and be re-armed, with twin 15-inch replacing the triple 11-inch turrets, but all work on her was abandoned after she sustained further severe damage from air attack.

Displacement: 31,800 tons (38,900 tons full).

Dimensions: 741½(wl) 771(oa) × 100 × 27/32½ feet.

Machinery: Twelve Wagner boilers (pressure eight at 661 lb. and four at 735 lb.); three shafts; Brown-Boveri geared turbines, S.H.P. 160,000 = 32 knots.

Bunkers & Radius O.F. 6,300 tons; 10,000 miles at 19 knots.

Protection: Main w.l. belt 5 (fwd.)–12/13 (amid.)–3 (aft) inches. Upper deck 2 inches, main deck 3¼ (slope)–4¼ (flat) inches. Main turrets 4 (rear)–9¾ (side)–14¼ (face) inches, barbettes 14 inches, secondary turrets 6 inches. C.T. 14 inches.

Armament: Nine 11-inch (3 × 3), twelve 5.9-inch (4 × 2 and 4 × 1), fourteen 4.1-inch A.A. (7 × 2), sixteen 37mm. A.A. (8 × 2) guns; six 21-inch T.T. (2 × 3); four aircraft and two catapults.

Complement: 1,800.

Notes: One catapult removed and eighteen 20mm. A.A. (1 × 4 and 7 × 2) guns added in *Scharnhorst*, and fourteen 20mm. A.A. (3 × 4 and 2 × 1) guns in *Gneisenau*.

Battleship TIRPITZ *showing elementary radar on mainmast*
Left: Battleships BISMARCK (*top*) *and* TIRPITZ (*bottom*)

Battleship BISMARCK *sailing on her only war cruise (20/5/41)*   [*Drüppel*

NAME	BUILDER	LAUNCHED	FATE
Bismarck	Blohm & Voss (Hamburg)	14.2.39	Gunfire R.N. battleships *King George V* and *Rodney*, and torpedoed cruiser *Dorsetshire*, aircraft (810, 818 & 820 Sqns.) of fleet carrier *Ark Royal*, and destroyers North Atlantic 27/5/41.
Tirpitz	Naval Dockyard (Wilhelmshaven)	1.4.39	Bombed R.A.F. aircraft (617 Sqn.) and capsized Tromso 12/11/44; scrapped *in situ* 1948.

Battleships: BISMARCK and TIRPITZ

The retention of secondary and tertiary batteries was an unusual feature of these vessels when most foreign contemporaries had adopted dual-purpose batteries for use against light surface craft and aircraft. This was probably accounted for by the fact that the standard 4.1-inch A.A. gun was considered too light for driving off light craft, whereas the United States Navy had adopted a 5-inch gun, and the Royal Navy a 5.25-inch or 4.5-inch gun for their dual-purpose batteries. The secondary battery was well disposed, in twin turrets, and the tertiary of sixteen A.A. guns, controlled by six high-angle directors, was unmatched anywhere. A fixed athwartship catapult was placed abaft the funnel, but a second to be placed abaft "B" turret, together with its hangar, was not finally put in. Only the *Tirpitz* carried two sets of torpedo tubes, mounted on the upper deck abaft the catapult.

Displacement: *Bismarck* 41,700 tons (50,900 tons full), *Tirpitz* 42,900 tons (52,600 tons full).

Dimensions: 794 (wl) 822¾(oa) × 118¼ × 28½/33½ except *Tirpitz* 29½/34¾ feet.

Machinery: Twelve Wagner boilers (pressure 808 lb.); three shafts; Brown-Boveri geared turbines, S.H.P. 138,000 = 29 knots.

Bunkers & *Bismarck* O.F. 7,900 tons; 8,100 miles at 19 knots. *Tirpitz* O.F .8,780 tons; 9,000 miles
Radius at 19 knots.

Protection: Main w.l. belt 12¾ inches, upper belt 2½ (fwd.)–5¾ (amid.)–3¼ (aft) inches, internal longitudinal bulkhead 1½–1¾ inches. Upper deck 2 (amid.)–3¼ (outer edge) inches, lower deck 3¼ (flat)–4½ (slope) inches, deck over magazines 3 inches and over steering gear 4¼ inches. Main turrets 7/14 (face)–6/8½ (side)–7/12½ (rear) inches and crown 5 inches, secondary turrets 1½ inches, barbettes 8½ (below UD)–13½ (above UD) inches. C.T. 14 inches.

Armament: Eight 15-inch (4 × 2), twelve 5.9-inch (6 × 2), sixteen 4.1-inch A.A. (8 × 2), sixteen 37mm. A.A. (8 × 2), *Bismarck* 36/*Tirpitz* 70–20mm. A.A. (4 × 4, 6 × 2 and 8 × 1/ 11 × 4, 16 × 2 and 10 × 1) guns; eight 21-inch (2 × 4) T.T. in *Tirpitz* only; six aircraft and one catapult.

Complement: *Bismarck* 2,200, *Tirpitz* 2,530.

NAME	BUILDER	LAUNCHED	FATE
"H"	Blohm & Voss (Hamburg)		Scrapped on slip 1940.
"J"	AG Weser (Bremen)		Scrapped on slip 1940.
"K"	,,		Projected.
"L"	Naval Dockyard (Wilhelmshaven)		Projected.
"M"	Blohm & Voss (Hamburg)		Projected.
"N"	Deutsche Werke (Kiel)		Projected.

The first two battleships of this class were laid down before even their final plans were completed, and when these were eventually drawn-up their size was increased by over 10,000 tons from that first envisaged. Nearly all this additional weight was put into hull strength and protection, which in turn required heavier double bottom plating than that already worked, while the armament was similar to that of the *Bismarck* and *Tirpitz* except that the calibre of the main guns was increased to 16-inch. To extend their radius diesel propulsion was adopted, and they were to be organised as support groups, able to keep the seas indefinitely, on which the raiding squadron could fall back when opposed by a heavier concentration Both the units laid down were broken up on the slips, by which time 1,200 tons had been worked into "H". and several hundred tons into "J", and the remainder were never started. The fixed athwartship catapult was placed across the quarterdeck, abaft "D" turret, and the aircraft stowed in an upper deck hangar placed between the after funnel and "C" turret: a neat arrangement that dispensed with high superstructure. They represented the culmination of German capital ship design, and had they been proceeded with would have inspired a new cycle of large and costly ships.

Displacement:	56,200 tons (68,000 tons full).
Dimensions:	872¾(pp) 912(oa) × 123¼ × 31½/36¾ feet.
Machinery:	Three shafts; M.A.N. diesel motors (four per shaft), B.H.P. 165,000 = 29 knots.
Bunkers & Radius	O.F. 10,000 tons; 16,000 miles at 19 knots.
Protection:	Main w.l. belt 12¾ inches, upper belt 2½ (fwd.)–6 (amid.)–1¼/3½ (aft) inches. Upper deck 2 inches, main deck 4 inches. Main turrets 9½ (rear)–14½ (side)–15½ (face) inches, barbettes 14½ inches, secondary turrets 4 inches. C.T. 15½ inches.
Armament:	Eight 16-inch (4 × 2), twelve 5.9-inch (6 × 2), sixteen 4.1-inch A.A. (8 × 2), sixteen 37mm. A.A. (8 × 2), twenty-four 20mm. A.A. (6 × 4) guns; six 21-inch (6 × 1–fixed and fwd.) T.T.; six aircraft and two catapults.
Complement:	2,600.

49

D

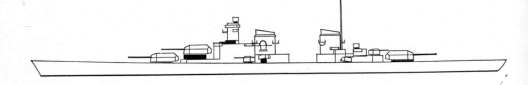

NAME	BUILDER	LAUNCHED	FATE
"O"	Deutsche Werke (Kiel)		Projected only.
"P"	Naval Dockyard) (Wilhelmshaven)		Projected only.
"Q"	Germania Werft (Kiel)		Projected only.

Battlecruisers: THREE projected

In the traditional manner these battlecruisers sacrificed armament and protection for speed and were real corsairs which, in spite of only mounting six main guns, could only have been successfully engaged by ships of capital rank. Their deck protection was nearly as strong as that of the battleships so that aircraft from a carrier group would have experienced great difficulty in inflicting bomb damage, but their A.A. armament of six guns and two high-angle directors was too light to withstand sustained attacks. A large radius of action was provided by diesel propulsion to the wing shafts, with which they could make 25 knots, while a turbine plant on the centre shaft only was brought in for full speed. No units of this class were laid down, and they were the final capital ship project to be seriously advanced.

Displacement:	32,300 tons (38,200 tons full).
Dimensions:	807(pp) 843¼(oa) × 98½ × 25/29½ feet.
Machinery:	Four Wagner boilers (pressure ... lb.); three shafts; M.A.N. diesel motors (four per wing shafts) and Brown-Boveri geared turbines (centre shaft), B.H.P. 110,000 + S.H.P. 60,000 = 33½ knots.
Bunkers & Radius	O.F. 5,100 tons; 14,000 miles at 19 knots.
Protection:	Main w.l. belt 7¼ inches, upper belt 3¾ inches. Upper deck 1¼ inches, main deck 3¼ inches, lower deck 4½ inches. Main turrets 8½ inches, barbettes 7¼ inches, secondary turrets ½ inch.
Armament:	Six 15-inch (3 × 2), six 5.9-inch (3 × 2), eight 4.1-inch A.A. (4 × 2), eight 37mm. A.A. (4 × 2), twenty 20mm. A.A. (5 × 4) guns; four aircraft and one catapult.
Complement:	1,900.

[*Drüppel*

*Stern view (above) and the after turrets (right) of the battle
ship* TIRPITZ

Launch of the aircraft carrier GRAF ZEPPELIN

[*Drüppel*

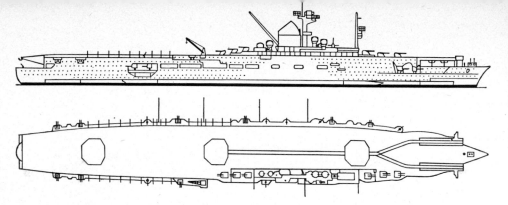

NAME	BUILDER	LAUNCHED	DATE
Graf Zeppelin	Deutsche Werke (Kiel)	8.12.38	Construction suspended 1940, resumed to modified design 1942, again suspended 1943; scuttled Stettin 25/4/45, salved and Russian; mined 15m. north of Rügen 15/8/47.
Unnamed	Germania Werft (Kiel)		Scrapped incomplete on slip 1940.

Aircraft carriers filled a vital role either operating with, or in support of, the raiding squadrons in providing fighter air cover, and strike and reconnaissance aircraft. But ship, rather than aircraft, features predominated in the design and cut back aircraft capacity. The heavy A.A. armament of twelve guns, controlled by four high-angle directors, amply met defensive requirements but their disposition, all along the starboard side, was open to criticism. It restricted flight deck operations when engaging air targets to port, and was an undue concentration more easily liable to disruption by only localised damage. In view of the extra high speed steaming undertaken by carriers when operating their aircraft, the radius of action was on the short side, while, to aid manoeuvrability, two Voith-Schneider cycloidal propellers, powered by electric motors, were fitted forward. As neither of these vessels were finally completed two further 12,000-ton carriers, which had only been contemplated pre-war were not further advanced.

Displacement:	23,200 tons (32,600 tons full).
Dimensions:	820$\frac{1}{4}$(wl) 862$\frac{3}{4}$(oa) $\times$ 103$\frac{1}{4}$ $\times$ 21/26$\frac{1}{2}$ feet (flight deck 790 $\times$ 118$\frac{3}{4}$ feet).
Machinery:	Sixteen Lamont boilers (pressure 1,249 lb.); four shafts; Brown-Boveri geared turbines, S.H.P. 200,000 = 33$\frac{3}{4}$ knots.
Bunkers & Radius	O.F. 6,400 tons; 8,000 miles at 19 knots.
Protection:	Main w.l. belt 4 inches. Flight deck $\frac{3}{4}$ inch, main deck 1$\frac{1}{2}$ (flat)–2$\frac{1}{2}$ (slope) inches. Casemates and barbettes 1$\frac{1}{2}$ inches, turrets $\frac{1}{2}$ inch.
Armament:	Sixteen 5.9-inch (8 $\times$ 2), twelve 4.1-inch A.A. (6 $\times$ 2), twenty-two 37mm. A.A. (11 $\times$ 2), twenty-eight 20mm. A.A (28 $\times$ 1) guns; forty aircraft and two catapults.
Complement:	1,760.
Notes:	Full load displacement increased to 34,000 tons after 1942 modification.

Light cruiser EMDEN

[*Drüppel*

NAME	BUILDER	LAUNCHED	FATE
Emden	Naval Dockyard (Wilhelmshaven)	7.1.25	Scuttled Heikendorfer Bight 3/5/45 after being bombed R.A.F. aircraft Kiel 14/4/45; scrapped 1947.

In the absence of any design studies undertaken in the years immediately following the First World War, this vessel was developed from the latest proven design with which war experience was available. The draft provision to have the main guns twin-mounted on the centre line was not implemented, and single mountings were shipped in these positions supplemented by four single mountings on the broadside. For active employment during the Second World War the *Emden* lacked sufficient A.A. guns and deck protection and was principally employed on minelaying and training duties.

Displacement: 5,600 tons (6,990 tons full).
Dimensions: 492¼(pp) 508½(oa) × 47 × 19/21¾ feet.
Machinery: Ten Marine boilers (pressure 235 lb.); two shafts; Blohm & Voss geared turbines, S.H.P. 46,500 = 29 knots.
Bunkers & Radius O.F. 1,266 tons; 5,300 miles at 18 knots.
Protection: Main belt 2 inches, decks ¾ inch (upper and main), gunshields ½–¾ inch, C.T. 3 inches.
Armament: Eight 5.9-inch (8 × 1), three 3.5-inch A.A. (3 × 1), four 37mm. A.A. (4 × 1) guns; four 21-inch (2 × 2) T.T.; one hundred and twenty mines.
Complement: 630.
Notes: At least four 20mm. A.A. (1 × 4) guns, if not more, were added.

Light cruiser KÖLN *with full heavy A.A. armament of six 3.5-inch guns*   [*Drüppel*

NAME	BUILDER	LAUNCHED	FATE
Karlsruhe	Deutsche Werke (Kiel)	20.8.27	Torpedoed R.N. submarine *Truant* south of Christiansand 10/4/40.
Köln	Naval Dockyard (Wilhelmshaven)	23.5.28	Bombed 8th U.S.A.A.F. aircraft Wilhelmshaven 30/3/45; scrapped 1946.
Königsberg	,,	26.3.27	Bombed R.N. aircraft (800 & 803 Sqns.) Bergen 10/4/40; salved 1943, capsized 22/9/44 and abandoned.

Light Cruisers: KARLSRUHE, KÖLN, and KÖNIGSBERG

Although these cruisers were intended to operate with the raiding squadrons, and introduced mixed turbine and diesel propulsion to extend their radius, the weight of armament carried heavily loaded the hull, and the position of the forward turret and bridge represented a concentration of weight forward which prejudiced seakeeping qualities. The heavy A.A. guns were first mounted singly aft, then paired on the centre line, and finally—with the addition of a further twin mounting—the two forward mountings were winged out. The *Karlsruhe* was the only unit refitted pre-war when the fore funnel was heightened, caps added to both funnels, a heavier tripod mainmast added abaft the after funnel, and was externally bulged, which added much needed beam.

Displacement:	6,650 tons (8,130 tons except *Karlsruhe* 8,350 tons full).
Dimensions:	554½(wl) 570¾(oa) × 50¼ except *Karlsruhe* 54½ (over bulges) × 17¾/21¼ feet.
Machinery:	Six Marine boilers (pressure 235 lb.); two shafts; Germania (*Karlsruhe*) Blohm & Voss (*Köln*) or Schichau (*Königsberg*) geared turbines and M.A.N. diesel motors, S.H.P. 68,000 + B.H.P. 1,800 = 32 except *Karlsruhe* 30 knots.
Bunkers & Radius	O.F. 1,145 + 261 tons; 5,200 miles at 19 knots.
Protection:	Main w.l. belt 2 inches. Main deck ¾ inch. Main turrets and barbettes 1¼ inches, secondary turrets ½ inch. C.T. 3 inches.
Armament:	Nine 5.9-inch (3 × 3), six 3.5-inch A.A. (3 × 2), eight 37mm. A.A. (4 × 2), four 20mm A.A. (4 × 1) guns; twelve 21-inch (4 × 3) T.T.; two aircraft and one catapult.
Complement:	820.
Notes:	At least four 20mm. A.A. (1 × 4) guns, if not more, were added in *Köln*, the aircraft and catapult were removed, and the after bank of torpedo tubes on each side were taken out and the hull plated over.

Light cruiser KÖNIGSBERG *as completed with 3.5-inch A.A. guns in single mountings aft* [*Drüppel*

Light cruiser KARLSRUHE *as completed* (right) *and after 1939 refit* (below)

[*Drüppel*

Light cruiser LEIPZIG *with aircraft and catapult forward of the funnel* [*Drüppel*

NAME	BUILDER	LAUNCHED	FATE
Leipzig	Naval Dockyard (Wilhelmshaven)	18.10.29	Scuttled south-west of Lister 20/7/46.

Light Cruiser: LEIPZIG

A modification of the "Königsberg" class with 3-feet more beam, both after turrets placed on the centre line, the funnels trunked into a single uptake positioned nearly amidships with the aircraft catapult placed forward of it, a third shaft added for a more powerful cruising diesel installation, and the main belt extended forward and aft.

Displacement:	6,710 tons (8,290 tons full).
Dimensions:	544½(pp) 580¾(oa) × 53¼ × 17/21¾ feet.
Machinery:	Eight Marine boilers (pressure 235 lb.); three shafts; Parsons geared turbines (wing shafts) and M.A.N. diesel motors (four on centre shaft), S.H.P. 66,000 + B.H.P. 12,400 = 32 knots.
Bunkers & Radius	O.F. 1,183 + 348 tons; 5,700 miles at 19 knots.
Protection:	Main w.l. belt 2 inches. Main deck ¾ (flat)–1 (slope) inch. Main turrets and barbettes 1¼ inches, secondary turrets ½ inch. C.T. 2 inches.
Armament:	Nine 5.9-inch (3 × 3), six 3.5-inch A.A. (3 × 2), eight 37mm. A.A. (4 × 2), ten 20mm. A.A. (2 × 4 and 2 × 1) guns; twelve 21-inch (4 × 3) T.T.; two aircraft and one catapult.
Complement:	850.
Notes:	Six T.T. removed in 1941, and the remainder in 1944, together with the forward boiler room, when converted for training duties, and *ca.* ten 20mm. A.A. (2 × 4 and 2 × 1) guns added.

Light cruiser NÜRNBERG *with aircraft and catapult abaft the funnel*   [*Drüppel*

NAME	BUILDER	LAUNCHED	FATE
Nürnberg	Deutsche Werke (Kiel)	8.12.34	Russian *Admiral Makarov* (1946).

Light Cruiser: NÜRNBERG

A further modification of the "Königsberg" class and *Leipzig* with the hull lengthened and main belt extended to the stem, the heavy A.A. armament further augmented and moved more amidships instead of being concentrated aft, the single trunked funnel moved further forward and the aircraft catapult resited abaft it, and a light mizzen mast added.

Displacement: 6,980 tons (8,380 tons full).
Dimensions: 557¾(pp) 593¾(oa) × 53¾ × 16½/21 feet.
Machinery: Eight Marine boilers (pressure 235 lb.); three shafts; Parsons geared turbines (wing shafts) and M.A.N. diesel motors (four on centre shaft), S.H.P. 60,000 + B.H.P. 12,400 = 32 knots.
Bunkers & Radius O.F. 1,100 + 348 tons; 5,700 miles at 19 knots.
Protection: Main w.l. belt 2 inches. Main deck ¾ (slope)–1 (flat) inch. Main turrets and barbettes 1¼ inches, secondary turrets ½ inch. C.T. 3 inches.
Armament: Nine 5.9-inch (3 × 3), eight 3.5-inch A.A. (4 × 2), eight 37mm. A.A. (4 × 2), four 20mm. A.A. (4 × 1) guns; twelve 21-inch (3 × 4) T.T.; two aircraft and one catapult
Complement: 896.
Notes: Catapult and two after banks of T.T. removed, and A.A. armament augmented by addition of two 37mm. and twenty-nine 20mm. (2 × 4, 10 × 2 and 1 × 1) guns.

E

Effective camouflage of light cruiser NÜRNBERG

[*Drüppel*

Right: Heavy cruiser ADMIRAL HIPPER (*top*) *as completed, and sister vessel* BLÜCHER (*bottom*) *as modified with clipper stem and funnel cap*

Heavy cruiser ADMIRAL HIPPER

NAME	BUILDER	LAUNCHED	FATE
Admiral Hipper	Blohm & Voss (Hamburg)	6.2.37	Scuttled Heikendorfer Bight 3/5/45; scrapped 1946.
Blücher	Deutsche Werke (Kiel)	8.6.37	Torpedoed and gunfire shore batteries Drobak 9/4/40.

Heavy Cruisers: ADMIRAL HIPPER and BLÜCHER

The German Navy was late in the field of heavy cruiser construction, but benefited by the much publicised shortcomings of earlier foreign cruisers of this type. In spite of being intended for raiding operations only turbine machinery was fitted, and their radius reduced in consequence, which proved an embarrassment during war operations. They were well protected, for their type, with the belt continued to the bows. The heavy A.A. was good and was enhanced by the ultimate provision of four high-angle directors, but only the superimposed turrets were fitted with rangefinders for the 8-inch guns. The *Admiral Hipper* was completed with a vertical stem and only two high-angle directors forward but later embodied the clipper stem, had two more high-angle directors put in aft, and a funnel cap added—all as in *Blücher*. The catapult was placed aft, over the after end of the hangar.

Displacement:	13,900 tons (18,600 tons full).
Dimensions:	639¾(wl) 675¾(oa) × 70 × 19/25¼ feet.
Machinery:	Twelve Lamont (pressure 1,175 lb.—*Admiral Hipper*), or Wagner (pressure 1,028 lb.—*Blücher*) boilers; three shafts; Blohm & Voss (*Admiral Hipper*) or AG Weser (*Blücher*) geared turbines, S.H.P. 132,000 = 32½ knots.
Bunkers & Radius	O.F. 4,250 tons; 6,800 miles at 19 knots.
Protection:	Main w.l. belt 3¼ inches. Upper deck 1¼ inches, main deck 1¼ (flat)–2½ (slope) inches. Main turrets 6½ inches, barbettes 3¾ inches, secondary turrets ½ inch. C.T. 2 inches. Externally bulged.
Armament:	Eight 8-inch (4 × 2), twelve 4.1-inch A.A. (6 × 2), twelve 37mm. A.A. (6 × 2), four 20mm. A.A. (4 × 1) guns; twelve 21-inch (3 × 4) T.T.; three aircraft and one catapult
Complement:	1,600.
Notes:	About four 20mm. A.A. (4 × 1) guns were added in *Blücher*, while thirty-five 20mm. A.A. (8 × 2 and 3 × 1) guns were added in *Admiral Hipper*.

Heavy cruiser PRINZ EUGEN   [*Drüppel*

NAME	BUILDER	LAUNCHED	FATE
Prinz Eugen	Germania Werft (Kiel)	22.8.38	U.S.N. (1946); expended as target Kwajalein 15/11/47.
Seydlitz	AG Weser (Bremen)	19.1.39	Construction halted 1942 and converted to aircraft carrier, scuttled incomplete Königsberg 10/4/45, salved and Russian *Poltava*; construction abandoned 1950.
Lützow	,,	1.7.39	Russian (1940), completion abandoned 5/41, bombed German aircraft Leningrad 4/42, floating battery *Tallin* (1942). *Petropavlovsk* (1944) construction abandoned 1950.

Heavy Cruisers: LÜTZOW, PRINZ EUGEN, and SEYDLITZ

Generally similar to the "Admiral Hipper" class but with more pronounced clipper stem and funnel cap. The aircraft crane was moved further forward where it was less liable to mask the fire of the amidships heavy A.A. guns mounted on the upper deck, and in consequence the catapult was resited over the fore end of the hangar where the crane could plumb it. Provision was also made to carry 900 troops, all of which could be berthed in portable 3-tier bunks.

Of this group only the *Prinz Eugen* was completed; the *Lützow* was sold incomplete to the Russian Navy, who were never able to complete her; and the *Seydlitz* was converted to an aircraft carrier. How far this conversion progressed is not precisely known, but she is believed to have advanced to the stage of having her hull decked over.

Displacement:	14,800 tons (19,800 tons full).
Dimensions:	635(wl) 689(oa) × 71½ × 19/26 feet.
Machinery:	Twelve Wagner boilers (pressure 881 lb.) except *Prinz Eugen* Lamont boilers (pressure 1,012 lb.); three shafts; AG Weser except *Prinz Eugen* Brown-Boveri geared turbines, S.H.P. 132,000 = 32 knots.
Bunkers & Radius	O.F. 4,250 tons; 6,800 miles at 19 knots.
Protection:	Main w.l. belt 3¼ inches. Upper deck 1¼ inches, main deck 1¼ (flat)–2½ (slope) inches. Main turrets 6½ inches, barbettes 3¼ inches, secondary turrets ½ inch. C.T. 2 inches, D.C.T. 2 inches. Externally bulged.
Armament:	Eight 8-inch (4 × 2), twelve 4.1-inch A.A. (6 × 2), twelve 37mm. A.A. (6 × 2), eight 20mm. A.A. (2 × 4) guns; twelve 21-inch (3 × 4) T.T.; three aircraft and one catapult.
Complement:	1,600.
Notes:	Final light A.A. armament of *Prinz Eugen* comprised nineteen 37mm. (19 × 1) and eight 20mm. (2 × 4) guns. Boilers not pressed higher than 750 lb.

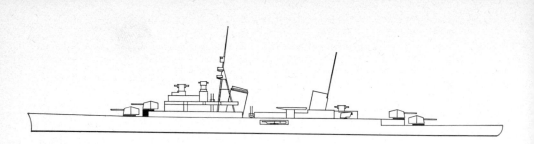

NAME	BUILDER	LAUNCHED	FATE
"M"	Deutsche Werke (Kiel)		Scrapped on slip 1941/3.
"N"	Naval Dockyard (Wilhelmshaven)		Scrapped on slip 1941/3.
"O"	Germania Werft (Kiel)		Scrapped on slip 1941/3.
"P"	,,		Cancelled.
"Q"	Schichau (Danzig)		Cancelled.
"R"	Deutsche Werke (Kiel)		Cancelled.

Light Cruisers: SIX projected

To secure speed and seaworthiness the armament in these vessels was reduced, compared to that carried in the earlier light cruisers, while the mixed turbine and diesel installation was retained for the necessary radius of action. But with only a single high-angle director and two twin heavy A.A. mountings they had little to offer in the way of air defence. The belt extended between the end barbettes, and was taken up to the level of the upper deck for the greater part of its length abreast the machinery spaces. Their large mine capacity indicated a further role well suited to their high speed for which they possessed ample gun power to ward off any interference from surface craft able to catch them. Only the first three ships of the class were laid down but were not greatly advanced before they were scrapped on the slips.

Displacement: 7,800 tons (10,400 tons full).

Dimensions: 584(wl) 600½(oa) × 55¾ × 19¾/23¾ feet.

Machinery: Four Wagner boilers (pressure 1,028 lb.); three shafts; Wagner geared turbines (wing shafts) + M.A.N. diesel motors (four on centre shaft), S.H.P. 100,000 + B.H.P. 16,500 = 35½ knots.

Bunkers & Radius O.F. 1,080 + 520 tons; 8,000 miles at 19 knots.

Protection: Main w.l. belt 2 inches. Main deck 1 (flat)–1½ (slope) inches. Main turrets ¾–3¼ (faces) inches, barbettes 1¼-2½ inches, secondary turrets ½ inch. C.T. 2 (crown)–4 (sides) inches.

Armament: Eight 5.9-inch (4 × 2), four 4.1-inch A.A. (2 × 2), eight 37mm. A.A. (4 × 2), four 20mm. A.A. (4 × 1) guns; eight 21-inch (2 × 4) T.T., one hundred and sixty mines; two aircraft and one catapult.

Complement: 920.

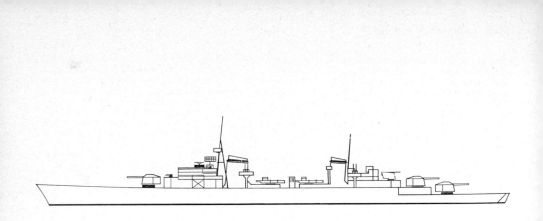

NAME	BUILDER	LAUNCHED	FATE
Sp.1 (ex-*Z.40*)	Germania Werft (Kiel)		Scrapped on slip . . /7/43.
Sp.2 (ex-*Z.41*)	,,		Cancelled 3/42.
Sp.3 (ex-*Z.42*)	,,		Cancelled 3/42.

Scout Cruisers: Sp.1–3.

The cancellation of the 7,800-ton light cruisers left those capital ships already completed devoid of any screen as none of the existing light cruisers could match them for prolonged high speed steaming, and the heavy cruisers were short on endurance. As a temporary expedient an enlarged destroyer design was proposed with the addition of a third centre shaft to which a powerful diesel installation was coupled. By this means their radius was increased to 25–33 per cent above that possessed by the battleships *Bismarck* and *Tirpitz*: an ample margin for their purpose. The concentration of the gun armament aft left no doubt of their course of action on sighting the enemy, and they could not hope to press home a reconnaissance. The old axim that armour. not speed, was vision could, perhaps, be disregarded to some extent now that RDF was available, but unfortunately its development in the German Navy was not so marked as in the American and British navies. Under these circumstances the employment of fast, but unarmoured, small scouts was problematical, but the dilemma was resolved by the premature loss of the *Bismarck*, the crippling effect this had on the employment of the *Tirpitz*, and the scout cruiser project was abandoned after the initial unit only had been laid down.

Displacement: 4,542 tons (5,900 tons full).
Dimensions: 475¾(wl) 498¾(oa) × 48 × 15/18¼ feet.
Machinery: Four Wagner boilers (pressure 1,028 lb.); three shafts; Wagner geared turbines (wing shafts) + M.A.N. diesel motors (four on centre shaft), S.H.P. 77,500 + B.H.P. 14,500 = 36 knots.
Bunkers & Radius O.F. 1,102 + 250 tons; 12,000 miles at 19 knots.
Protection: Longitudinal bulkheads (amid) ¾ inch. Upper deck (amid) ¾ inch, main turrets 1 inch, barbettes ½ inch, secondary turret ½ inch.
Armament: Six 5.9-inch (3 × 2), two 3.5-inch A.A. (1 × 2), eight 37mm. A.A. (4 × 2), twelve 20mm. A.A. (3 × 4) guns; ten 21-inch (2 × 5) T.T., one hundred and forty mines.
Complement: 583

Heavy cruiser PRINZ EUGEN, *note radar on fore director tower and external DG coil round hull* [*Drüppel*

Right: Destroyers Z.3 (MAX SCHULTZ) *and* Z.5 (PAUL JACOBI). *Hull numbers indicate flotilla and position in flotilla. During the war the light A.A. armament of the latter was increased to fourteen 37mm. (7 × 2) and thirteen 20mm. (6 × 2 and 1 × 1) guns while "C" gun, at the fore end of the after shelter deck, was removed.*

[*Drüppel*

NAME	BUILDER	LAUNCHED	FATE
Z.1 (*Leberecht Maass*)	Deutsche Werke (Kiel)	18.8.35	Bombed in error German aircraft north-west of Borkum 22/2/40.
Z.2 (*Georg Thiele*)	,,	18.8.35	Scuttled Rombaksfjord 13/3/40.
Z.3 (*Max Schultz*)	,,	30.11.35	Bombed in error German aircraft north-west of Borkum 22/2/40.
Z.4 (*Richard Beitzen*)	,,	30.11.35	R.N. *H.97* (1945); sold C. W. Dorkin, scrapped Gateshead 10/1/49.
Z.5 (*Paul Jacobi*)	AG Weser (Bremen)	24.3.36	R.N. (1945), French *Desaix* (1946); scrapped 1954.
Z.6 (*Theodor Riedel*)	,,	22.4.36	R.N. (1945), French *Klèber* (1946); scrapped 1958.
Z.7 (*Hermann Schoemann*)	,,	16.7.36	Gunfire R.N. cruiser *Edinburgh* Arctic 2/5/42.
Z.8 (*Bruno Heinemann*)	,,	15.9.36	Mined English Channel 25/1/42.
Z.9 (*Wolfgang Zenker*)	Germania Werft (Kiel)	27.3.36	Scuttled Rombaksfjord 13/4/40.
Z.10 (*Hans Lody*)	,,	14.5.36	R.N. *R.38* (1945); scrapped Sunderland 1949.
Z.11 (*Bernd von Arnim*)	,,	8.7.36	Scuttled Rombaksfjord 13/4/40.
Z.12 (*Erich Giese*)	,,	12.3.37	Scuttled Ofotfjord 13/4/40.
Z.13 (*Erich Koellner*)	,,	18.3.37	Scuttled Ofotfjord 13/4/40.
Z.14 (*Friedrich Ihn*)	Blohm & Voss (Hamburg)	5.11.35	Russian *Zorki* (1946); scrapped 1961.
Z.15 (*Erich Steinbrinck*)	,,	24.9.36	Russian *Pylki* (1946); scrapped 1961.
Z.16 (*Friedrich Eckoldt*)	,,	21.3.37	Gunfire R.N. cruiser *Sheffield* off Bear Island 31/12/42.

In building up the destroyer flotillas the underlying principle was to offset quantity by quality, and consequently the first series of destroyers were among the largest in the world. The design was one of robust simplicity—with an adequate but not outstanding armament for their tonnage—except for the main machinery where the adoption of very high boiler pressures did not prove a great success. The need to augment the A.A. armament led to the eventual removal of "C" gun and the addition of several light pieces, mounted overall, but to no uniform pattern in individual ships. By the end of the war Z.5, in addition to the two twin 37mm. mountings originally carried abreast the after funnel, mounted a twin 20mm. on the foc's'le, a twin 20mm. before and two twin 37mm. abaft "B" gun, two twin 20mm. in the bridge wings, two twin 37mm. in lieu of "C" gun, one twin 37mm. and two twin 20mm. on the shelter between "C" and "D" guns, and a single 20mm. abaft "D" gun—a total of fourteen 37mm. and thirteen 20mm. As completed they had vertical stems but Z.4 and Z.5 were lengthened in 1944 when they were given clipper stems.

Displacement:	Z.1–4: 2,232 tons (3,156 tons full); Z.5–8: 2,171 tons (3,100 tons full); Z.9–13: 2,270 tons (3,190 tons full); Z.14–16: 2,239 tons (3,165 tons full).
Dimensions:	374(pp) 390$\frac{1}{2}$(oa) except Z.9–16 380$\frac{1}{2}$(pp) 397(oa) × 37 × 12$\frac{1}{2}$/14 feet.
Machinery:	Six Wagner (pressure 1,028 lb.) except Z.9–16 Benson (pressure 1,616 lb.) boilers; two shafts; Wagner geared turbines, S.H.P. 70,000 = 38 knots except Z.1–4 38$\frac{1}{4}$ knots.
Bunkers & Radius	O.F. 752 tons; 4,400 miles at 19 knots.
Armament:	Five 5-inch (5 × 1), four 37mm. A.A. (2 × 2) guns; eight 21-inch (2 × 4—sixteen torpedoes) T.T.; sixty mines.
Complement:	325.

Destroyer z.14 (FRIEDRICH IHN)   [*Drüppel*

Right: Destroyer z.6 (THEODOR RIEDEL) *with national markings on shield to "B" gun*

The light A.A. armament of these vessels was considerably augmented during the war. Although "C" gun was removed to compensate for the additional topweight there was no reduction in the torpedo armament.

81

F

Destroyers z.20 (GEORG THIELE—*above*) *and* z.15 (ERICH STEINBRINCK—*below*)　　　　[*Drüppel*

Destroyer z.24 (above) and flotilla leader z.28 (below). The latter vessel, although belonging to the type 1936A, was not designed to ship a twin turret forward, and had additional accommodation fitted at the fore end of the after shelter deck.

[*Drüppel*

Destroyer KARL GALSTER (Z.20) *illustrating the less prominent clinker screens fitted to this class* [*Drüppel*

NAME	BUILDER	LAUNCHED	FATE
Z.17 (*Diether von Roeder*)	AG Weser (Bremen)	19.8.37	Scuttled Rombaksfjord 13/4/40.
Z.18 (*Hans Lüdemann*)	,,	1.12.37	Scuttled Rombaksfjord 13/4/40.
Z.19 (*Hermann Künne*)	,,	22.12.37	Scuttled Rombaksfjord 13/4/40 after being torpedoed R.N. destroyer *Eskimo*.
Z.20 (*Karl Galster*)	,,	15.6.38	Russian *Protschny* (1946).
Z.21 (*Wilhelm Heidkamp*)	,,	20.8.38	Torpedoed R.N. destroyers .... Narvik 10/4/40.
Z.22 (*Anton Schmitt*)	,,	20.9.38	Torpedoed R.N. destroyers .... Narvik 10/4/40.

These vessels were generally similar to the preceding class except that the last three units, Z.20–22, were completed with clipper stems. The extra buoyancy so provided forward improved seaworthiness and was adopted for all subsequent construction. The overloading and frequent breakdowns of the high pressure boilers under arduous war steaming conditions led to the forming of a special committee, before the end of 1939, to enquire into the problem. The sole surviving unit of this class after 1940, the Z.20, was altered similarly to the earlier vessels and had two 37mm. A.A. (1 × 2) and twelve 20mm. A.A. (1 × 4, 3 × 2 and 2 × 1) guns added.

Displacement:	2,411 tons (3,415 tons full).
Dimensions:	$393\frac{3}{4}$(wl) $403\frac{1}{2}$(oa) except *Z.20–22* 410(oa) × $38\frac{3}{4}$ × $12\frac{1}{2}/14\frac{3}{4}$ feet.
Machinery:	Six Wagner boilers (pressure 1,028 lb.); two shafts; Wagner geared turbines, S.H.P. 70,000 = 38 knots.
Bunkers & Radius	O.F. 760 tons; 4,850 miles at 19 knots.
Armament:	Five 5-inch (5 × 1), four 37mm. A.A. (2 × 2) guns; eight 21-inch (2 × 4—sixteen torpedoes) T.T.; sixty mines.
Complement:	323.

Destroyer z.25 as
French HOCHE

[*Drüppel*

NAME	BUILDER	LAUNCHED	FATE
Z.23	AG Weser (Bremen)	15.12.39	Scuttled La Pallice 21/8/44 after being bombed R.A.F. aircraft.
Z.24	,,	7.3.40	Driven ashore rocke fire R.A.F. aircraft Le Verdon 25t/8/44.
Z.25	,,	16.3.40	R.N. (1945), French *Hoche* (1946).
Z.26	,,	2.4.40	Gunfire R.N. cruiser *Trinidad* and destroyer *Eclipse* North Sea 29/3/42
Z.27	,,	1.8.40	Gunfire R.N. cruisers *Enterprise* and *Glasgow* Bay of Biscay 28/12/43.
Z.28	,,	20.8.40	Bombed Allied aircraft Sassnitz 6/3/45.
Z.29	,,	15.10.40	U.S.N. (1945); scuttled Skagerak 1946.
Z.30	,,	8.12.40	R.N. (1945); expended as experimental vessel 1948.

With this class the calibre of the main guns was increased to 5.9-inch and the two forward guns housed in a turret except in Z.28, fitted as a flotilla leader, which had single mountings throughout and had "C" gun suppressed for additional accommodation. To compensate for this additional weight of armament the hull dimensions were slightly enlarged, but on nowhere near an adequate scale, and the twin turret cramped internal arrangements and weakened the hull structure forward. Owing to the shortage of twin 5.9-inch turrets only a single gun was mounted forward on completion together with additional light A.A. guns before the bridge. The twin turret was available from the end of 1942 and was fitted to all except Z.26, but shortly afterwards "C" gun was removed so that further light A.A. guns could be added. Typical of this class were Z.25 and Z.29 which had one 20mm. on the fo'c'sle, two twin 20mm. A.A. mountings abaft the turret, two twin 37mm. before the bridge, two twin 20mm. in the bridge wings, two twin and two single 37mm. around the after funnel, two single 37mm. in lieu of "C" gun, and two quadruple 20mm. on the deckhouse forward of "D" gun which, with "C" gun out, had been extended to the fore end of the after shelter deck, and one 20mm. at the after end.

Displacement:	2,603 tons (3,605 tons full except Z.29 and 30 3,597 tons full) except Z.25–27 2,543 tons (3,543 tons full) and Z.28 2,596 tons (3,519 tons full).
Dimensions:	393½ (pp) 400¼ (wl) 416¾ (oa) × 39¼ × 12¾/15 feet.
Machinery:	Six Wagner boilers (pressure 1,028 lb.); two shafts; Wagner geared turbines, S.H.P. 70,000 = 38½ knots.
Bunkers & Radius:	O.F. 752 tons except Z.28 804 tons and Z.29 and 30 825 tons; 5,000 miles except Z.28 5,800 miles and Z.29–30 5,900 miles at 19 knots.
Armament:	Five except Z.28 four 5.9-inch (1 × 2 and 3 × 1 except Z.28 4 × 1), six 37mm. A.A. (2 × 2 and 2 × 1) guns; eight except Z.28 seven 20mm. A.A. (2 × 4 except Z.28 1 × 2 and 5 × 1), eight 21-inch (2 × 4—sixteen torpedoes) T.T.; sixty mines.
Complement:	321 except Z.28 327.

Destroyer z.26 as completed with only single 5.9-inch gun on fo'c'sle [*Drüppel*

Destroyer z.33 with twin 5.9-inch gun turret forward

[*Drüppel*]

Destroyer Z.34 with full 5.9-inch gun armament [*Drüppel*]

TYPE	BUILDER	LAUNCHED	FATE
Z.31	AG Weser (Bremen)	15.5.41	R.N. (1945), French *Marceau* (1946); scrapped 1956.
Z.32	,,	15.8.41	Driven ashore gunfire R.C.N. destroyers *Haida* and *Huron*, Ushant 9/6/44.
Z.33	,,	15.9.42	Russian *Provorny* (1946).
Z.34	,,	5.5.42	U.S.N. (1945); scuttled Skagerak 26/3/46.
Z.37	Germania Werft (Kiel)	24.2.41	Scuttled Bordeaux 24/8/44.
Z.38	,,	5.8.41	R.N. *Nonsuch* (1945); scrapped 1949.
Z.39	,,	2.12.41	U.S.N. *DD.939* (1945); French (1948) and cannibalised for spares and used as floating pier.

Destroyer type 1963A(Mob): Z.31–34 and Z.37–39

Generally similar to the preceding class and only *Z.31* was completed without the twin turret forward. This was, however, installed in 1944, only to be removed the following year, when undergoing damage repairs, and replaced by a single 4.1-inch A.A. and additional light A.A. guns. The final armament carried by *Z.31* was three 5.9-inch (3 × 1) all aft, one 4.1-inch A.A. forward, two single and two twin 37mm. A.A. before the bridge, two 20mm. A.A. in the bridge wings, four single 37mm. A.A. around the after funnel, and two single 37mm. A.A. and one quadruple 20mm. A.A. between "C" and "D" guns on the after shelter deck. As completed Z.33 and Z.34 had a light A.A. armament of four 37mm. (2 × 2) and twenty-one 20mm. (2 × 4, 2 × 2, and 7 × 1) guns but only carried four reloads for the T.T.

Displacement:	2,603 tons (3,597 tons full).
Dimensions:	400¼(wl) 416¾(oa) × 39¼ × 12¾/15 feet.
Machinery:	Six Wagner boilers (pressure 1,028 lb.); two shafts; Wagner geared turbines, S.H.P. 70,000 = 38½ knots.
Bunkers & Radius	O.F. 825 tons; 5,900 miles at 19 knots.
Armament:	Five 5.9-inch (1 × 2 and 3 × 1), six 37mm. A.A. (2 × 2 and 2 × 1), eight 20mm. A.A. (2 × 4) guns; eight 21-inch (2 × 4—sixteen torpedoes) T.T.; sixty mines.
Complement:	321 except *Z.32–34* 320.

Destroyer z.43 reverted to 5-inch guns [*Drüppel*

TYPE	BUILDER	LAUNCHED	FATE
Z.35	AG Weser (Bremen)	2.10.42	Mined Gulf of Finland 12/12/44.
Z.36	,,	15.5.43	Mined Gulf of Finland 12/12/44.
Z.40–42	Germania Werft (Kiel)	—	See under scout cruisers *Sp.1–3.*
Z.43	AG Weser (Bremen)	9.43	Scuttled Geltinger Bight 3/5/45 after being mined and bombed Allied aircraft; salved and scrapped 1953.
Z.44	,,	20.1.44	Bombed Allied aircraft Bremen 29/7/44; scuttled incomplete 20/7/46.
Z.45	,,	1944	Suspended 1944; scuttled incomplete 20/7/46.

Destroyer type 1936B: Z.35 & 36 and Z.43–45

The adoption of 5.9-inch guns had not, on the whole, been a complete success, as the additional weight carried, especially with the twin turret concentration forward, had been to the detriment of seakeeping qualities despite slightly increased but inadequate hull dimensions. Not only that, the need to supplement the light A.A. armament had resulted in a critical weight problem entailing the removal of at least one 5.9-inch gun so that the weight of the broadside remained virtually unaffected in spite of shipping a heavier calibre gun. Therefore, this class reverted to the lighter 5-inch gun, all in single mountings, and the designed light A.A. armament was improved to include six 37mm. (2 × 2 and 2 × 1) around the after funnel, and thirteen 20mm. (3 × 4 and 1 × 1) mounted in the wings of the upper bridge and aft together with a solitary mounting on the fo'c'sle.

Displacement:	2,527 tons (3,507 tons full).
Dimensions:	400¼(wl) 416¾(oa) × 39¼ × 11½/14 feet.
Machinery:	Six Wagner boilers (pressure 1,028 lb.); two shafts; Wagner geared turbines, S.H.P. 70,000 = 38 knots.
Bunkers & Radius	O.F. 825 tons; 5,900 miles at 19 knots.
Armament:	Five 5-inch (5 × 1), six 37mm. A.A. (2 × 2 and 2 × 1), thirteen 20mm. A.A. (3 × 4 and 1 × 1) guns; eight 21-inch (2 × 4—sixteen torpedoes) T.T.; seventy-six mines.
Complement:	321.

Destroyer type 1938Ac: Z.40–42
See under scout cruisers *Sp.1–3*.

Destroyer type 1936C: Z.46–50

This class was generally similar to the earlier types but with the gun armament completely re-arranged following the introduction of a new 5.1-inch D.P. gun twin-mounted in turrets. The turrets were disposed one forward and two aft, the three 37mm. A.A. twin mountings were placed one before the bridge and two abreast the after funnel, and the four twin 20mm. A.A. mountings in wing positions on the bridge and abaft the after funnel. The addition of an RDF-fitted high-angle director at the fore end of the shelter deck considerably enhanced the A.A. capabilities of the main guns.

Displacement: 2,574 tons (3,594 tons full).
Dimensions: 397(wl) 413½(oa) × 40 × 11¾/14½ feet.
Machinery: Six Wagner boilers (pressure 1,028 lb.); two shafts; Wagner geared turbines, S.H.P. 70,000 = 37½ knots.
Bunkers & Radius O.F. 860 tons; 6,000 miles at 19 knots.
Armament: Six 5.1-inch D.P. (3 × 2), six 37mm. A.A. (3 × 2), eight 20mm. A.A. (4 × 2) guns; eight 21-inch (2 × 4—sixteen torpedoes) T.T.; sixty mines.
Complement: 320.

NAME	BUILDER	LAUNCHED	FATE
Z.46	AG Weser (Bremen)	—	Bombed Allied aircraft Bremen while building and scrapped on slip 1945.
Z.47	,,	—	Bombed Allied aircraft Bremen while building and scrapped on slip 1945.
Z.48–50	,,	—	Cancelled.

Destroyer type 1942: Z.51

This vessel was an uncompleted prototype which introduced diesel main propulsion to destroyers to secure the extended radius dictated in staff requirements for operations in Northern waters. The hull form closely resembled that of the type 1938B project, which was never put into production, except that a raised fo'c'sle was added in view of the more severe weather conditions experienced in Northern waters. Primarily a floating test bed to examine the feasibility of the installed machinery, the armament was of almost secondary consideration and included the new 5.1-inch D.P. gun, in four single mountings, equally disposed fore and aft, four twin 37mm. A.A. mountings placed abreast the two funnels, and three quadruple 20mm. mountings, two before the bridge and one aft: an improved arrangement, nevertheless, than before. But the lack of a high-angle director would not have enabled the 5.1-inch guns to be fought very effectively as A.A. weapons. This heavy gun armament, for her size, was partly compensated for by reductions in the torpedo armament and mine load.

Displacement: 2,053 tons (2,632 tons full).
Dimensions: 354¼(pp) 374(oa) × 36 × 12¼/14½ feet.
Machinery: Three shafts; M.A.N. diesels (one per wing shafts and four on centre shaft), B.H.P. 57,120 = 36 knots.
Bunkers & O.F. 551 tons; 13,500 miles at 19 knots.
Radius
Armament: Four 5.1-inch (4 × 1), eight 37mm. A.A. (4 × 2), twelve 20mm. A.A. (3 × 4) guns; six 21-inch (2 × 3) T.T.; fifty mines.
Complement: 235.

NAME	BUILDER	LAUNCHED	FATE
Z.51	AG Weser (Bremen)	1944	Bombed Allied aircraft Bremen while building and construction suspended; scrapped.

Destroyer type 1942C: Z.52–56

This was the final, and largest, destroyer design put into production. None were ever completed and their performance, therefore, cannot be assessed, but if it matched their symmetry they would have proved most successful vessels. They were outstanding in both main propulsion and armament, and also adopted diesel main propulsion for unmatched radius with no appreciable loss of speed as compared with the turbine-engined destroyers. The main guns were the new 5.1-inch D.P., again twin-mounted in three turrets, but this time placed two forward and one aft, and controlled by RDF-fitted high-angle directors mounted on the bridge and aft. New and heavier calibre light A.A. guns were also incorporated: three single 55mm. around the after funnel, and seven twin 30mm., with three mountings on the bridge, two abreast the fore funnel, and two aft. In spite of the heavy gun armament there was no reduction in the torpedo armament or the mine load which equalled that of earlier types.

Displacement: 2,818 tons (3,703 tons full).
Dimensions: 413½(wl) 433(oa) × 41¼ × 13½/16 feet.
Machinery: Two shafts; M.A.N. diesel motors (four per shaft), B.H.P. 76,000 = 37½ knots.
Bunkers & O.F. 630 tons; 16,000 miles at 19 knots.
  Radius
Armament: Six 5.1-inch D.P. (3 × 2), three 55mm. A.A. (3 × 1), fourteen 30mm. A.A. (7 × 2) guns; eight 21-inch (2 × 4) T.T.; sixty mines.
Complement: 320.

NAME	BUILDER	LAUNCHED	FATE
Z.52–56	AG Weser (Bremen)	—	Cancelled 1944/5.
Z.57 and 58	Germania Werft (Kiel)	—	Cancelled 1945.

Destroyer type 1945:

Project for high performance type which reverted to geared turbines and sacrificed radius for speed. They were to be solely gun-armed and were provided fore and aft with RDF-fitted high-angle directors.

Displacement: 2,657 tons (3,700 tons full).
Dimensions: 397(wl) 413½(oa) × 39¼ × 12¾/15 feet.
Machinery: Six Wagner boilers (pressure 1,028 lb.); two shafts; Wagner geared turbines, S.H.P. 80,000 = 40 knots.
Bunkers & Radius O.F. 800 tons; 3,600 miles at 19 knots.
Armament: Eight 5.1-inch D.P. (4 × 2), four 55mm. A.A. (4 × 1), twelve 30mm. A.A. (6 × 2) guns; eight 21-inch (2 × 4—16 torpedoes) T.T.; one-hundred mines.
Complement: 365.

Destroyer type 1938B:

This was a pre-war mass production project that was not followed-up to provide long range destroyers able to accompany the raiding squadrons. The design was kept simple to ease production, and embodied a flush-decked hull of moderate dimensions with the main guns arranged in twin turrets fore and aft. The turrets afforded shelter for guns crews as under ocean conditions they would have been subject to the penalties of exposure with a corresponding loss of efficiency at the guns.

Displacement: 1,971 tons (2,747 tons full).
Dimensions: 354¼(wl) 367½(oa) × 37 × 10½/13 feet.
Machinery: Four Wagner boilers (pressure 1,028 lb.); two shafts; Wagner geared turbines, S.H.P. 50,000 = 36½ knots.
Bunkers & Radius O.F. 563 tons; 9,500 miles at 19 knots.
Armament: Four 5-inch (2 × 2), one 37mm. A.A., two 20mm. A.A. (2 × 1) guns; eight 21-inch (2 × 4) T.T.
Complement: 239.

G

NAME	BUILDER	LAUNCHED	FATE
ZH.1 (ex-*Gerard Callenburgh*)	Rotterdam D.D.	12.10.39	Scuttled Rotterdam 14/5/40, salved and German (1942); gunfire R.N. destroyers *Ashanti* and *Tartar* 20 m. × north-west Ile de Batz 9/6/44.
ZF.2 (ex-*Opiniatre*)	Fges. & Ch. de la Gironde (Bordeaux)		Retroceded incomplete 1945 and scrapped.
ZG.3 (ex-*Vasilevs Georgios I*)	Yarrow (Scotstoun)	3.3.38	Scuttled Piraeus 20/4/41, salved and German *Hermes*, (1943); scuttled west of La Goulette 7/5/43 after being bombed by Allied aircraft.
ZN.4 (ex-　　　)	Naval Dockyard (Horten)	1941	*TA.7* (1941), sabotaged while building 1945, retroceded incomplete R.N.N. *Aalesund* (1945); construction abandoned 1950.
ZN.5 (ex-　　　)	,,	1941	*TA.8* (1941), sabotaged while building 1945, retroceded incomplete 1945 and scrapped.

Ex-R.Neth.N. destroyer: ZH.1

1,204 tons (2,228 tons full): $344\frac{1}{2}$(pp) $347\frac{3}{4}$(oa) $\times$ $34\frac{3}{4}$ $\times$ $9\frac{1}{4}/11\frac{1}{2}$ feet: three Yarrow boilers (pressure 412 lb.), two-shafts, Werkspoor geared turbines S.H.P. 49,500 = $37\frac{1}{2}$ knots, O.F. 560 tons (5,400 miles at 19 knots): five 4.7-inch (2 $\times$ 2 and 1 $\times$ 1), four 37mm. A.A. (2 $\times$ 2), four 20mm. A.A. (1 $\times$ 4) guns, eight 21-inch (2 $\times$ 4) T.T.: complement 236.

Ex-French destroyer: ZF.2

2,070 tons (2,910 tons full): $333\frac{1}{4}$(pp) 371(oa) $\times$ $36\frac{1}{2}$ $\times$ $8\frac{1}{2}/11\frac{1}{4}$ feet: four Indret boilers (pressure 412 lb.), two-shafts, Rateau geared turbines S.H.P. 58,000 = 37 knots, O.F. 820 tons (4,700 miles at 19 knots): five 5-inch (1 $\times$ 2 & 3 $\times$ 1), four 37mm. A.A. (2 $\times$ 2), ten 20mm. A.A. (1 $\times$ 4 and 6 $\times$ 1) guns, eight 21-inch (2 $\times$ 4) T.T.: complement 245.

Notes: Was originally armed with six 5.1-inch (3 $\times$ 2), four 37mm. A.A. (2 $\times$ 2), four 13mm A.A. (2 $\times$ 2) guns, seven 21.7-inch (1 $\times$ 3 and 2 $\times$ 2) T.T.

Ex-R.H.N. destroyer: ZG.3

1,414 tons (2,008 tons full): 312(pp) $331\frac{1}{4}$(oa) $\times$ $33\frac{1}{2}$ $\times$ $8\frac{1}{2}/10\frac{1}{2}$ feet: three Yarrow boilers (pressure 235 lb.), two-shafts, Parsons geared turbines S.H.P. 34,000 = 36 knots, O.F. 455 tons (4,800 miles at 19 knots): four 5-inch (4 $\times$ 1), four 37mm. A.A. (4 $\times$ 1), four 20mm. A.A. (4 $\times$ 1) guns, eight 21-inch (2 $\times$ 4) T.T.: complement 220.

Ex-R.N.N. destroyers: ZN.4 and 5

1,278 tons (1,694 tons full): 300(pp) 328(oa) $\times$ $34\frac{3}{4}$ $\times$ $8\frac{3}{4}/10\frac{1}{2}$ feet: three Yarrow boilers (pressure 470 lb.), two-shafts, De Laval geared turbines S.H.P. 30,000 = 34 knots, O.F. 300 tons (3,100 miles at 19 knots): four 4.7-inch (1 $\times$ 2 and 2 $\times$ 1), two 37mm. A.A. (1 $\times$ 2), six 20mm. A.A. (6 $\times$ 1) guns, four 21-inch (1 $\times$ 4) T.T.: complement 162.

NAME	BUILDER	LAUNCHED	FATE
Pfeil (ex-*T.139*, ex-*S.139*)	Schichau (Elbing)	12.11.06	Target service.
Komet (ex-*T.151*, ex-*V.151*)	Vulcan (Stettin)	14.9.07	Target service, T.R.V.; U.S.N. (1945); scrapped Netherlands 1949.
Eduard Jungmann (ex-*T.153*, ex-*V.153*)	,,	13.11.07	Gunnery school tender, T.R.V.; U.S.N. (1945); scrapped Netherlands 1949.
T.155 (ex-*V.155*)	,,	28.1.08	Submarine tender, T.R.V.; scuttled Swinemüude 22/4/45.
T.156 (ex-*V.156*)	,,	29.2.08	Submarine tender, T.R.V.; scuttled Kiel 3/5/45.
T.157 (ex-*V.157*)	,,	29.5.08	Submarine tender, T.R.V.: mined New Waterway 22/10/43.
T.158 (ex-*V.158*)	,,	23.6.08	Submarine tender, T.R.V.; Russian *Prozorlivi* (1945).
Blitz (ex-*T.185*, ex-*V.185*)	,,	9.4.10	Target service; Russian *Vystrel* (1945).
Claus von Bevern (ex-*T.190*, ex-*V.190*)	,,	12.4.11	Experimental vessel; scuttled Skagerak 1946.

Torpedo boat: PFEIL
530 tons (685 tons full): $230\frac{1}{4}$(pp) 232(oa) $\times$ $25\frac{1}{2}$ $\times$ $10/10\frac{1}{2}$ feet: Schultz Thornycroft boilers (pressure 280 lb.), two shafts, reciprocating (VTE) I.H.P. 11,000 = 30 knots, O.F. 200 tons (3,000 miles at 17 knots): disarmed: complement 87.

Torpedo boats: KOMET, EDUARD JUNGMANN, T.155–158
660 tons except *Komet* 675 tons (800 tons full): $237\frac{3}{4}$(pp) $242\frac{1}{4}$(oa) $\times$ $25\frac{1}{2}$ $\times$ $10\frac{1}{4}/10\frac{1}{2}$ feet: four Schultz boilers (pressure 280 lb.), two shafts, reciprocating (VTE) I.H.P. 10,900 = 30 knots, O.F. 181 tons (3,500 miles at 17 knots): one 3.5-inch, one 20mm. A.A. except *Komet* and *E. Jungmann* disarmed: complement 87.

Torpedo boat: BLITZ
761 tons (858 tons full): $241\frac{1}{2}$(pp) $242\frac{1}{2}$(oa) $\times$ $25\frac{3}{4}$ $\times$ $10\frac{1}{2}/10\frac{3}{4}$ feet: three Schultz-Thornycroft boilers (pressure 265 lb.), two shafts, A.E G. turbines S.H.P. 17,750 = 30 knots, O.F. 198 tons (1,400 miles at 17 knots): disarmed: complement 87.

Torpedo boat: CLAUS VON BEVERN
755 tons (860 tons full): $241\frac{1}{2}$(pp) $242\frac{1}{2}$(oa) $\times$ 26 $\times$ $10/10\frac{1}{2}$ feet: three Schultz Thornycroft boilers (pressure 265 lb.), two shafts, AEG-Vulcan turbines S.H.P. 18,000 = $30\frac{1}{2}$ knots, O.F. 198 tons (1,400 miles at 17 knots): one 4.1-inch, two 20mm. A.A. (2 $\times$ 1) guns: complement 99.

Torpedo boat: T.196
755 tons (875 tons full): $241\frac{1}{2}$(pp) $242\frac{3}{4}$(oa) $\times$ $26\frac{1}{4}$ $\times$ $10\frac{1}{2}/10\frac{3}{4}$ feet: three Schultz-Thornycroft boilers (pressure 265 lb.), two shafts, Germania turbines S.H.P. 18,200 = $32\frac{1}{2}$ knots, O.F. 204 tons (1,850 miles at 19 knots): two 4.1-inch (2 $\times$ 1), two 20mm. A.A. (2 $\times$ 1) guns: complement 99.

EDUARD JUNG-MANN, *old torpedo boat used as a gunnery tender*

[*Drüppel*

NAME	BUILDER	LAUNCHED	FATE
T.196 (ex-*G196*)	Vulcan (Stettin)	24.5.11	Fleet tender; Russian *Pronzitelny* (1945).
T.107 (ex-*G.7*)	Germania Werft (Kiel)	7.11.11	Torpedo school tender, T.R.V.; Russian *Poraschayuschy* (1945).
T.108 (ex-*G.8*)	,,	21.12.11	Torpedo school tender; R.N. (1945) and scrapped.
T.110 (ex-*G.10*)	,,	15.3.12	Torpedo school tender; scuttled Travemünde 5/5/45.
T.111 (ex-*G.11*)	,,	23.4.12	Torpedo school tender; scuttled after bomb damage Kiel 3/5/45.

Torpedo boats: T.107, 108, 110 and 111

760 tons (885 tons full): 247¾(pp) 249¾(oa) × 25 × 10½/10½ feet: three Schultz-Thornycroft boilers (pressure 265 lb.), two shafts, Germania turbines S.H.P. 16,000 = 31 knots, O.F. 173 tons (1,900 miles at 17 knots): one 4.1-inch, two 20mm. A.A. (2 × 1) guns, three 19.7-inch (1 × 3—*T.108* and *110*) or three 21-inch (1 × 3) and one 19.7-inch (*T.107* and *T.111*) T.T.: complement 85.

Notes: Were lengthened by 14¾ feet 1928/31.

т.107 *torpedo school tender later used as a TRV*

[*Drüppel*

CLAUS VON BEV-ERN, *old torpedo boat used as an experimental vessel*

[*Drüppel*

Torpedo boat ALBATROS *as completed bore a marked resemblance to First World War design*   [Drüppel]

Left: Destroyers z.37 (*top*) *and* z.38 (*bottom as* R.N. NONSUCH) *both with full* 5·9-*inch armament and twin turret forward.   Note external DG coil following line of upper deck*   [Drüppel]

Torpedo boat GREIF *with light A.A. armament not shipped forward of after funnel* [*Drüppel*]

NAME	BUILDER	LAUNCHED	FATE
Albatros	Naval Dockyard (Wilhelmshaven)	15.7.26	Gunfire R.N.N. minelay *Olav Tryggvason* Oslofjord 10/4/40.
Falke	,,	22.9.26	Bombed R.A.F. aircraft Le Havre 14/6/44.
Greif	,,	15.7.26	Bombed Allied aircraft Seine estuary 25/5/44.
Kondor	,,	22.9.26	Scuttled Le Havre 28/6/44 after being bombed R.A.F. aircraft.
Möwe	,,	24.3.26	Bombed R.A.F. aircraft Le Havre 14/6/44.
Seeadler	,,	15.7.26	Torpedoed R.N. M.T.B. north of Boulogne 13/5/42.

Torpedo boat type 1923: ALBATROS, FALKE, GREIF, KONDOR, MÖWE and SEEADLER

The design of these boats generally followed that of the latest craft built during the First World War (types V.125–130, S.131–139, and H.140–147) and although dimensions were enlarged, to make them more weatherly, they were still inclined to be wet owing to the absence of sheer and lack of freeboard. Novel constructional features were longitudinal framing and a double bottom to the hull outside of the machinery spaces. The low bridge accentuated the height of the tall fore funnel, which ensured that smoke was carried well clear, but it was later necessary to raise the bridge level. The lead ship of the class, the *Möwe*, was slightly shorter and beamier than the remainder. Whereas the fo'c'sle and quarterdeck guns were placed behind shields, the superfiring gun aft was on an open high-angle mounting, and the light A.A. armament was augmented, during the war, by the addition of one 37mm. and four 20mm. (1 × 4) guns.

Displacement: 924 tons (1,290 tons full).
Dimensions: 278¾(pp) 288¾(oa) except *Möwe* 285½(oa) × 27¼ except *Möwe* 27¾ × 9½/11½ feet
Machinery: Three Marine boilers (pressure 264 lb.); two shafts; *Albatros* & *Kondor* Schichau, *Falke* & *Greif* Vulcan, *Möwe* Blohm & Voss, and *Seeadler* Germania geared turbines, S.H.P. 23,000 = 33 knots except *Möwe* 32 knots.
Bunkers & O.F. 340 tons; 3,100 miles at 17 knots.
Radius
Armament: Three 4.1-inch (3 × 1), two 20mm. A.A. (2 × 1) guns; six 21-inch (2 × 3) T.T.
Complement: 122.

[*Drüppel*

Torpedo boat GREIF *after 1927 with additions to bridge, mainmast moved aft and rigged with boat boom, and "X" gun made super-firing*

In the torpedo boat TIGER *the boats are stowed farther forward, abreast the fore funnel, than in the earlier class which carried them abreast the after funnel*

Torpedo boat LEOPARD *mounted 5-inch guns*   [*Drüppel*

NAME	BUILDER	LAUNCHED	FATE
Iltis	Naval Dockyard (Wilhelmshaven)	12.10.27	Torpedoed R.N. MTB .... north of Boulogne 13/5/42.
Jaguar	,,	15.3.28	Bombed R.A.F. aircraft Le Havre 14/6/44.
Leopard	,,	15.3.28	Lost collision with *Preussen* Skagerak 30/4/40.
Luchs	,,	15.3.28	Torpedoed R.N. submarine *Swordfish* North Sea 26/7/40.
Tiger (i)	,,	15.3.28	Lost collision with Z.3 (*Max Schultz*) east of Bornholm 25/8/39.
Wolf	,,	12.10.27	Mined north of Dunkerque 8/1/41.

Torpedo boat type 1924: ILTIS, JAGUAR, LEOPARD, LUCHS, TIGER (i), and WOLF

Similar to the preceding class except that the hull was lengthened by about 15 feet and the beam slightly increased. Two units, the *Leopard* and *Luchs*, mounted heavier calibre 5-inch guns, which were later adopted for destroyers. The light A.A. armament was increased during the war by the addition of one 37mm. and two 20mm. (2 × 1) guns.

Intervening between this and the previous class, which were originally rated as destroyers, was a 200-ton torpedo boat project which was not advanced as no useful craft could be produced within such a limited parameter.

Displacement: 933 tons (1,320 tons full).
Dimensions: 292(pp) 305(oa) × 28½ × 9¼/11½ feet.
Machinery: Three Marine boilers (pressure 264 lb.); two shafts; *Iltis* & *Tiger* Vulcan, *Jaguar* & *Luchs* Schichau, and *Leopard* & *Wolf* Brown Boveri geared turbines, S.H.P. 23,000 = 33 knots.
Bunkers & Radius O.F. 380 tons; 3,100 miles at 17 knots.
Armament: Three 4.1-inch except *Leopard* and *Luchs* 5-inch (3 × 1), two 20mm. A.A. (2 × 1) guns; six 21-inch (2 × 3) T.T.
Complement: 123.

Torpedo boat ILTIS *pre-war*

[*Drüppel*

Right: Torpedo boat T.8 *as completed with only a slightly raked stem*

[*Drüppel*

H

NAME	BUILDER	LAUNCHED	FATE
T.1	Schichau (Elbing)	1938	Bombed Allied aircraft Kiel 10/4/45.
T.2	,,	1938	Bombed U.S.A.A.F. aircraft Bremen 29/7/44: salved 1944 and scrapped Cuxhaven 1945.
T.3	,,	1938	Bombed R.A.F. aircraft Le Havre 19/9/40, salved 1941; mined north of Hela 14/3/45.
T.4	,,	1938	U.S.N. (1945), R.D.N. (1947); for disposal 1951.
T.5	AG Weser (Bremen)	22.11.37	Mined north of Hela 14/3/45.
T.6	,,	16.12.37	Mined west of Shetlands 7/11/40.
T.7	,,	18.6.38	Bombed U.S.A.A.F. aircraft Bremen 29/7/44; salved and scrapped 1945.
T.8	,,	10.8.38	Scuttled Strander Bight (Kiel) 3/5/45.
T.9	Schichau (Elbing)	1939	Scuttled Strander Bight (Kiel) 3/5/45.
T.10	,,	1939	Bombed R.A.F. aircraft Gdynia 18/12/44.
T.11	AG Weser (Bremen)	1.3.39	R.N. (1945), French *Bir Hakeim* (1946); for disposal 1949.
T.12	,,	12.4.39	Russian *Podvischny* (1946).

Torpedo boat T.1 *had two banks of triple T.T. but only a single gun*

[*Drüppel*

Torpedo boat type 1935:
T.1–12

These boats were diminutives of the earlier classes, sacrificed gunpower to retain both banks of torpedo tubes, and were over 2 knots faster but with a more limited radius. They were lengthened, during the war, to 285½(oa) feet by the addition of a clipper stem, one 40mm. A.A. gun replaced the after set of torpedo tubes, and six 20mm. A.A. (6 × 1) guns were added.

Displacement: 844 tons (1,088 tons full) except *T.9–12* 839 tons (1,082 tons full).
Dimensions: 269(wl) 275½(oa) × 28¼ × 7½/9½ feet.
Machinery: Four Wagner boilers (pressure 1,028 lb.); two shafts: Wagner geared turbines, S.H.P. 31,000 = 35½ knots.
Bunkers & O.F. 205 tons; 2,400 miles at 19 knots.
Radius
Armament: One 4.1-inch, three 20mm. A.A. (3 × 1) guns; six 21-inch (2 × 3) T.T.; thirty mines.
Complement: 119.

Torpedo boat T.11 *showing box-shaped bridge which was a feature of this class* [*Drüppel*

Torpedo boat T.17 *fitted for minelaying*

[*Drüppel*

Torpedo boat type 1937: T.13–21

Practically repeats of the preceding class but with a slightly increased radius of action and 37mm. in lieu of 20mm. A.A. guns. The light A.A. armament was augmented during the war by replacing the after set of torpedo tubes by one 40mm. gun, and the addition of one 37mm. and ten 20mm. (2 × 4 and 2 × 1) guns.

NAME	BUILDER	LAUNCHED	FATE
T.13	Schichau (Elbing)	15.6.39	Bombed Allied aircraft Kattegat 10/4/45.
T.14	,,	1939	U.S.N. (1945), French *Dompaire* (1947); discarded 1949.
T.15	,,	1939	Bombed U.S.A.A.F. aircraft Kiel 13/12/43.
T.16	,,	1940/1	Paid-off Frederikshavn 13/4/45 after being bombed Allied aircraft; scrapped.
T.17	,,	1940/1	Russian *Porivisty* (1946).
T.18	,,	1940/1	Bombed Russian aircraft Gulf of Finland 17/9/44.
T.19	,,	1941	U.S.N. (1945), R.D.N. (1947); discarded 1951.
T.20	,,	...10.41	R.N. (1945), French *Baccarat* (1946); discarded 1949.
T.21	,,	..11.41	U.S.N. (1945); scuttled Skagerak 1946.

[*Drüppel*

Torpedo boat T.36 *with augmented light A.A. armament: a 37mm. bowchaser has been added, two single 20mm. in the bridge wings, a 40mm. shipped in lieu of the after T.T. with two quadruple 20mm. mountings forward and abaft it*

Displacement:	853 tons (1,098 tons full).
Dimensions:	269(wl) 278¾(oa) × 29¼ × 8¼/10¼ feet.
Machinery:	Four Wagner boilers (pressure 1,028 lb.); two shafts; Wagner geared turbines, S.H.P. 31,000 = 35½ knots.
Bunkers & Radius	O.F. 216 tons; 3,000 miles at 19 knots.
Armament:	One 4.1-inch, two 37mm. A.A. (2 × 1) guns; six 21-inch (2 × 3) T.T.; thirty-eight mines.
Complement:	119.

NAME	BUILDER	LAUNCHED	FATE
T.22	Schichau (Elbing)	1941	Mined Narva Bay 18/8/44.
T.23	,,	...11.41	R.N. (1945), French *Alsacien* (1946).
T.24	,,	...11.41	Driven ashore rocket fire of R.A.F. aircraft Le Verdon 24/8/44.
T.25	,,	1942	Gunfire R.N. cruisers *Enterprise* and *Glasgow* Bay of Biscay 28/12/43.
T.26	,,	1942	Gunfire R.N. cruisers *Enterprise* and *Glasgow* Bay of Biscay 28/12/43.
T.27	,,	1942	Driven ashore gunfire R.C.N. destroyers *Haida* off Ushant 29/4/44, and torpedoed R.N. MTB and R.A.F. aircraft 7/5/44.
T.28	,,	...11.41	R.N. (1945), French *Lorrain* (1946).
T.29	,,	...11.41	Gunfire R.N. destroyers *Ashanti*, R.C.N. *Athabaskan*, *Haida* and *Huron* off Ushant 26/4/44.
T.30	,,	1943	Mined Narva Bay 18/8/44.
T.31	,,	1943	Mined and torpedoed Russian MTB Gulf of Finland 20/6/44.
T.32	,,	1944	Mined Narva Bay 18/8/44.
T.33	,,	1943	Russian *Primierny* (1946).
T.34	,,	1944	Mined west of Arkona 20/11/44.
T.35	,,	1944	U.S.N. DD.935 (1945), French (1947) and cannibalised for spares.
T.36	,,	1944	Mined and bombed Allied aircraft off Swinemünde 4/5/45.

Torpedo boat T.26 *as completed*

[*Drüppel*

Torpedo boat type 1939: T.22–36

The shortcomings of the two previous classes in possessing mainly a torpedo armament and little else was that, except for minelaying, their operational scope was limited to use against ship targets. Consequently, an adequate gun armament was incorporated in this class which enabled them to be more flexibly employed. As they were completed after hostilities had broken out they benefited from war experience and carried a more numerous light A.A. armament from the onset.

Displacement: 1,294 tons (1,754 tons full).
Dimensions: 318¼(wl) 334¾(oa) × 32¾ × 8½/10½ feet.
Machinery: Four Wagner boilers (pressure 1,028 lb); two shafts; Wagner geared turbines, S.H.P 32,000 = 33½ knots.
Bunkers & Radius O.F. 401 tons; 5,000 miles at 19 knots.
Armament: Four 4.1-inch (4 × 1), four 37mm. A.A. (2 × 2), nine except *T.23* and *24* seven 20mm. A.A. (1 × 4 and 3/5 × 1), two 15mm. A.A. (2 × 1) guns; six 21-inch (2 × 3) T.T.; fifty mines.
Complement: 198.

Fleet torpedo boat type 1941: T.37–51

Closely similar to the preceding class but with the bridge structure modified to include a low-angle director for the main guns, the light A.A. armament more advantageously re-grouped, and the radius of action was increased. Only the first three units, T.37–39, nearly approached completion.

Displacement: 1,493 tons (2,155 tons full).
Dimensions: $334\frac{3}{4}$(wl) $347\frac{3}{4}$(oa) × $33\frac{1}{4}$ × $9\frac{1}{2}/12\frac{1}{4}$ feet.
Machinery: Four Wagner boilers (pressure 1,028 lb.); two shafts; Wagner geared turbines, S.H.P. 40,000 = 34 knots.
Bunkers & Radius: O.F. 582 tons; 6,500 miles at 19 knots.
Armament: Four 4.1-inch (4 × 1); six 37mm. A.A. (3 × 2), eight 20mm. A.A. (1 × 4 and 2 × 2) guns; six 21-inch (2 × 3) T.T.
Complement: 210.

NAME	BUILDER	LAUNCHED	FATE
T.37	Schichau (Elbing)	1945	Scuttled Bremerhaven 1945.
T.38	,,	,,	Scuttled Kiel 1945.
T.39	,,	,,	Scuttled Kiel 1945.
T.40	,,	,,	Scuttled incomplete Elbing 3/45.
T.41	,,	,,	Scuttled incomplete Elbing 3/45.
T.42	,,	,,	Scuttled incomplete Elbing 3/45.
T.43	,,	,,	Scuttled incomplete Elbing 3/45.
T.44–51	,,		Destroyed on slip Elbing 3/45.

Fleet torpedo boat type 1944: T.52–60

Although essentially similar to the two preceding classes the design was recast to embrace a long fo'c'sle deck with the break positioned abaft the after funnel, the 4.1-inch were placed in twin A.A. mountings controlled by a high-angle director on the bridge, the light A.A. armament was a homogeneous battery of ten 30mm. (5 × 2) guns, and speed was increased at the expense of the radius. This class never advanced further than the planning stage and none were ever laid down.

Displacement: 1,418 tons (1,794 tons full).
Dimensions: 321½(wl) 338(oa) × 33¼ × 9½/12¼ feet.
Machinery: Four Wagner boilers (pressure 1,028 lb.); two shafts; Wagner geared turbines, S.H.P. 52,000 = 37¼ knots.
Bunkers & Radius O.F. 300 tons; 4,500 miles at 19 knots.
Armament: Four 4.1-inch A.A. (2 × 2), ten 30mm. A.A. (5 × 2) guns; six 21 inch (2 × 3) T.T.
Complement: 214.

NAME	BUILDER	LAUNCHED	FATE
T.52–60	Schichau (Elbing)		Cancelled.

NAME	BUILDER	LAUNCHED	FATE
T.61	Wilton-Fijenoord (Schiedam)	...6.44	Capsized on launching and salved: torpedoed incomplete while in tow by Allied aircraft off West Frisian Islands 13/9/44.
T.62	,,		Destroyed on slip Rotterdam. 1944
T.63	Rotterdam D.D.	28.10.44	Scuttled incomplete Kiel 2/5/45
T.64	,,		Destroyed on slip Rotterdam. 1944
T.65	De Schelde (Flushing)	8.7.44	Scuttled incomplete Kiel 1946.
T.66	,,		Bombed Allied aircraft while building 1944, and construction abandoned.
T.67	Wilton-Fijenoord (Schiedam)		Cancelled.
T.68	,,		Cancelled.
T.69	Rotterdam D.D.		Destroyed on slip Rotterdam.
T.70	,,		Destroyed on slip Rotterdam.
T.71	De Schelde (Flushing)		Cancelled.
T.72	,,		Cancelled.

Chronologically the design of these boats preceded that of the previous class, and was equally influenced by the material available, and that could be manufactured, in the Netherlands, where their construction was undertaken. Their advancement was hampered and retarded at every turn and although ordered late in 1940, only eight of the twelve were laid down by 1942 and, of these, only three reached launching stage. They broke away from the flush decked design and had a fo'c'sle deck, with the break just aft of the bridge, and the boiler rooms were all adjacent and their uptakes trunked into a single funnel. The 4.1-inch guns were equally disposed fore and aft with the inner mountings superimposed over the outer ones, two twin 37mm. A.A. mountings were placed abaft the funnel, four quadruple 20mm. A.A. mountings were winged out on the upper bridge and farther aft between the torpedo tubes, and control positions were provided fore and aft. They were the largest of the torpedo boats—and would have ranked as destroyers in any other navy—but had no opportunity to show their merits.

Displacement:	1,931 tons (2,566 tons full).
Dimensions:	361(wl) 374(oa) × 37 × 10½/12½ feet.
Machinery:	Three Yarrow boilers (pressure 411 lb.); two shafts; Werkspoor geared turbines, S.H.P. 49,500 = 35 knots.
Bunkers & Radius	O.F. 570 tons; 5,000 miles at 19 knots.
Armament:	Four 5-inch (4 × 1), four 37mm. A.A. (2 × 2), sixteen 20mm. A.A. (4 × 4) guns; eight 21-inch (2 × 4) T.T.
Complement:	223.

Torpedo boat
PANTHER

[*Drüppel*

NAME	BUILDER	LAUNCHED	FATE
Leopard (ex-*Balder*)	Naval Dockyard (Horton)	11.10.39	Retroceded 1945.
Löwe (ex-*Gyller*)	,,	2.7.38	Retroceded 1945.
Panther (ex-*Odin*)	,,	17.1.39	Retroceded 1945.
Tiger (ii) (ex-*Tor*)	Frederiksstad Mek. Verksted	9.9.39	Scuttled Frederiksstad 9/4/40, salved and German; retroceded 1945.

Ex-R.N.N. torpedo boats: LEOPARD, LÖWE, PANTHER, and TIGER

597 tons (708 tons full): 236$\frac{1}{4}$(pp) 243$\frac{3}{4}$(oa) × 25$\frac{1}{2}$ × 6$\frac{1}{2}$/9$\frac{1}{4}$ feet: three Yarrow boilers (pressure 450 lb.), two-shaft, De Laval geared turbines, S.H.P. 12,500 = 32 knots, O.F. 100 tons (3,500 miles at 15 knots): one 3.9-inch, two/four 20mm. A.A. (2/4 × 1), two 8mm. A.A. (2 × 1) guns, two 21-inch (1 × 2) T.T.: complement 72.

Notes: Were originally armed with three 3.9-inch (3 × 1) and one 40mm. A.A. guns. T.T. were later removed.

Minesweeper M.84, *note conspicuous boat gantry abaft funnel (see pages 137 and 139)*

[*Drüppel*

127

NAME	BUILDER	LAUNCHED	FATE
TF.1	Schichau (Elbing)	1942	
TF.2	,,	,,	Russian (1945).
TF.3	,,	,,	
TF.4	,,	,,	Russian (1945).
TF.5	,,	,,	Scuttled .... 5/45.
TF.6	,,	,,	Scuttled .... 5/45.
TF.7	,,	,,	
TF.8	,,	,,	

TFA.9 *was a former Royal Netherlands Navy torpedo boat*　　　　　　　　*[Drüppel*

Torpedo recovery vessels type 1942: TF.1–8

The provision of these vessels is in no way extraordinary, but what is unusual is the building of vessels of such high quality for this task, especially during war time when building and turbine blade cutting capacity were fully extended. In appearance they resembled small torpedo boats, and the first two groups closely resembled each other, except that the German built boats had the bridge structure faired into the funnel casing and had derricks at either end of the after deck, while the boats built in the Netherlands had their bridge sited slightly more forward and a less conspicuous funnel casing and only a single derrick amidships on the after deck. No boats of the third group were ever laid down.

Displacement:	381 tons (483 tons full).
Dimensions:	190¼(pp) 203½(oa) × 22 × 6¼/8 feet.
Machinery:	Two .... boilers (pressure ... lb.); two shafts; Schichau geared turbines, S.H.P. 6,000 = 23½ knots.
Bunkers & Radius	O.F. 71 tons; 2,000 miles at 19 knots.
Armament:	Two 20mm. A.A. (2 × 1) guns.
Complement:	61.
Notes:	Deck stowage for fourteen torpedoes.

I

NAME	BUILDER	LAUNCHED	FATE
TF.9	Netherlands Dock & Sbdg. (Amsterdam	1943/4	Russian (1945).
TF.10	,,	,,	Scuttled .... 5/45.
TF.11	,,	,,	Scuttled .... 5/45.
TF.12	,,	,,	Scuttled .... 5/45.
TF.13	Rotterdam D.D.	,,	Scuttled .... 5/45.
TF.14	,,	,,	Scuttled .... 5/45.
TF.15	Wilton-Fijenoord	,,	Russian (1945).
TF.16	,,	,,	Scuttled .... 5/45.
TF.17	,,	,,	Russian (1945).
TF.18	,,	,,	Scuttled .... 5/45.
TF.19	Rotterdam D.D.	,,	Scuttled .... 5/45.
TF.20	,,	,,	
TF.21	Van der Giessen (Krimpen)	,,	
TF.22	,,	,,	
TF.23	Netherlands Dock & Sbdg. (Amsterdam)	,,	
TF.24	,,	,,	
TF.25–36	Schichau (Elbing)		Cancelled.

Torpedo recovery vessels type 1943: TF.9–24

Displacement: 380 tons (491 tons full).
Dimensions: 190¼(pp) 203½(oa) × 22¼ × 6½/8 feet.
Machinery: Two .... boilers (pressure ... lb.); two shafts; Werkspoor geared turbines, S.H.P. 6,240 = 24 knots.
Bunkers & Radius O.F. 72 tons; 2,000 miles at 19 knots.
Armament: Two 20mm. A.A. (2 × 1) guns.
Complement: 61.
Notes: Deck stowage for fourteen torpedoes.

Torpedo recovery vessels type 1942: TF.25–36

Displacement: 473 tons (625 tons full).
Dimensions: 203½(pp) 216½(oa) × 26 × 6½/8¾ feet.
Machinery: Two .... boilers (pressure ... lb.); two shafts; Schichau geared turbines, S.H.P. 8,000 = 23½ knots.
Bunkers & Radius O.F. 120 tons; 3,200 miles at 19 knots.
Armament: One 37mm. A.A., four 20mm. A.A. (1 × 4) guns.
Complement: 76.
Notes: Deck stowage for fourteen torpedoes.

NAME	BUILDER	LAUNCHED	FATE
TFA.1 (ex-*Hogen*)	Naval Dockyard (Copenhagen)	1933	Heavily damaged when depot ship *Donau* blew-up Flensburg 14/6/45.
TFA.2 (ex-*Ornen*)	,,	19.10.34	Heavily damaged when depot ship *Donau* blew-up Flensburg 14/6/45.
TFA.3 (ex-*Glenten*)	,,	1933	Heavily damaged when depot ship *Donau* blew-up Flensburg 14/6/45.
TFA.4 (ex-*Dragen*)	,,	12.29	Mined Geltinger Bight 14/5/45.
TFA.5 (ex-*Hvalen*)	,,	1930	Heavily damaged when depot ship *Donau* blew-up Flensburg 14/6/45.
TFA.6 (ex-*Laxen*)	,,	,,	Heavily damaged when depot ship *Donau* blew-up Flensburg 14/6/45.
TFA.7 (ex-*Mewa*)	Gdynia	1935	
TFA.8 (ex-*Rybitwa*)	Modlin	26.4.35	
TFA.11 (ex-*Czajka*)	Modlin	10.4.35	*Westerplatte* (1942).
Oxhoft (ex-*Zuraw*)	Gdynia	22.8.38	Experimental vessel.
TFA.9 (ex-*G.16*)	Wilton-Fijennord (Schiedam)	1914	Scuttled Kiel 3/5/45 and scrapped.
TFA.10 (ex-*G.22*)	De Schelde (Flushing)	1904	Scuttled Kiel 5/45.

Ex-R.D.N. torpedo recovery vessels: TFA.1–3
290 tons (335 tons full): ....(pp) $198\frac{3}{4} \times 19\frac{1}{2} \times 7\frac{3}{4}/8\frac{1}{2}$ feet: two Thornycroft boilers (pressure ... lb.), two-shaft Atlas geared turbines, S.H.P. 6,000 = $27\frac{1}{2}$ knots, O.F. 40 tons (.,... miles at .. knots): two 3.5 inch (2 × 1), two 20mm. A.A. (2 × 1), two 8mm. A.A. (2 × 1) guns, six 18 inch (2 FB and 2 × 2) T.T.: complement 55.

Ex-R.D.N. torpedo recovery vessels: TFA.4–6
290 tons (335 tons full): ....(pp) $198\frac{3}{4}$(oa) $\times 19\frac{1}{2} \times 7\frac{3}{4}/8\frac{1}{2}$ feet: two Thornycroft boilers (pressure ... lb.), two-shaft Brown Boveri except *TFA.6* Atlas geared turbines, S.H.P. 6,000 = $27\frac{1}{2}$ knots, O.F. 40 tons (.,... miles at .. knots): two 3-inch (2 × 1), two 20mm. A.A. (2 × 1), two 8mm. A.A. (2 × 1) guns, eight 18-inch (2 FB and 2 × 2) T.T.: complement 51.
Notes: Former torpedo boats.

Ex-Polish torpedo recovery vessels: TFA.7, 8, 11 and OXHOFT
183 tons (... tons full): $139\frac{1}{2}$(pp) ....(oa) $\times 21\frac{1}{4} \times 5\frac{1}{2}/...$ feet: two-shaft .... diesel motors, B.H.P. 1,040 = 15 knots, O.F. ... tons (.,... miles at .. knots): one 3-inch gun: complement 30.
Notes: Former minesweepers.

Ex-R.Neth.N. torpedo recovery vessels: TFA.9
180 tons (230 tons full): $162\frac{1}{2}$(pp) ....(oa) $\times 17 \times 4\frac{1}{2}/5\frac{3}{4}$ feet: .... boilers (pressure ... lb.), two-shaft reciprocating (VTE) I.H.P. 2,600 = 25 knots, coal 44 tons (.,... miles at .. knots): two 3-inch (2 × 1) guns, three 17.7-inch (3 × 1) T.T.: complement 27.

Ex-R.Neth.N. torpedo recovery vessels: TFA.10
144 tons (185 tons full): $154\frac{1}{4}$(pp) ....(oa) $\times 16\frac{1}{2} \times 6/8$ feet: .... boilers (pressure ... lb.), one-shaft reciprocating (VC) I.H.P. 2,000 = 25 knots, coal 40 tons (1,230 miles at 8 knots): two 4 pdr. (2 × 1) guns, three 17.7-inch (3 × 1) T.T.: complement 24.
Notes: Former torpedo boats. Foc's'le was extended to abaft bridge and funnels trunked into a single casing. *TFA.10* had been removed from the effective list in 1930.

Minesweeper M.1 (*and also* M.2) *was fitted with Voith-Schneider cycloidal propellers, and these were later installed in* M.25–36. *Other units–except* M.3–24–*had their screws turning in Kort nozzles*

Left: Torpedo boat T.17 *with radar aerials on foremast*

NAME	BUILDER	LAUNCHED	FATE
M.1	C. Stülcken (Hamburg)	5.3.37	Bombed Allied aircraft Nordbyfjord 12/1/45.
M.2	,,	20.5.37	Rocket fire of R.A.F. aircraft Fedjefjord 11/3/45.
M.3	,,	28.9.37	Russian *T.901* (1945).
M.4	Oderwerke (Stettin)	16.10.37	U.S.N. (1945), French (1947); scrapped.
M.5	,,	16.10.37	Mined north-west of Christiansand 18/6/40.
M.6	,,	8.1.38	Mined off Lorient 30/11/41.
M.7	Flender Werft (Lubeck)	29.9.37	Russian *T.902* (1945).
M.8	,,	29.9.37	Torpedoed R.N. MTB's. off Hook of Holland 14/5/43.
M.9	,,	16.11.37	U.S.N. (1945), French *Somme* (1947); scrapped 1955.
M.10	C. Stülcken (Hamburg)	9.8.38	Gunfire R.N. surface forces off Lorient 14/3/44.
M.11	Oderwerke (Stettin)	23.8.38	Mined south-west of Norway 6/6/40.
M 12	Flender Werft (Lübeck)	6.8.38	U.S.N. (1945), French (1947); scrapped.
M.13	C. Stülcken (Hamburg)	28.2.39	Mined Gironde estuary 31/5/44.
M.14	C. Stülcken (Hamburg)	25.4.39	Mined off Swinemünde 3/5/45.

Minesweeper type 1935: M.1–260

The design of these vessels generally followed that of minesweepers of the First World War, but they were some 30 feet longer, oil-fired, and a little faster. When fitted for minelaying they could stow thirty mines and their displacement increased by some 60 tons. As they, and subsequent classes of mine-sweepers, were frequently pressed into service as escort vessels their gun armament received more attention than was demanded by their primary role, and was re-inforced by the addition of about six 20mm. A.A. (6 × 1) guns during the war. Cycloidal propellers were fitted in M.1 and M.2 only.

Displacement: 772 tons (874 tons full load up to M.24), 775 tons (878 tons full load from M.25 up).
Dimensions: 216½(pp) 224½(oa) × 27¼ × 7/8½ feet.
Machinery: Two Wagner or Lamont boilers (pressure 808 lb.); two shafts; reciprocating (VTE), I.H.P. 3,500 = 18¼ knots.
Bunkers & Radius O.F. 143 tons; 5,000 miles at 10 knots.
Armament: Two 4.1-inch A.A. (2 × 1), two 37mm. A.A. (2 × 1) guns.
Complement: 104.

NAME	BUILDER	LAUNCHED	FATE
M.15	C. Stülcken (Hamburg)	4.9.39	Bombed Allied aircraft Kiel 20/3/45.
M.16	,,	15.11.39	Bombed Allied aircraft Kiel 20/3/45; scrapped.
M.17	Oderwerke (Stettin)	29.7.39	Russian *T.903* (1945).
M.18	,,	16.9.39	Bombed Allied aircraft Kiel 20/3/45; scrapped.
M.19	,,	28.10.39	Bombed Allied aircraft Kiel 20/3/45; scrapped.

NAME	BUILDER	LAUNCHED	FATE
M.20	Flender Werft (Lübeck)	16. 6.39	Bombed Russian aircraft Narva Bay 20/7/44.
M.21	,,	6. 9.39	U.S.N. (1945), French (1947); scrapped.
M.22	,,	20. 3.40	Scuttled Kiel Canal 7/5/45.
M.23	,,	11. 7.40	Mined off Tallin 7/41, salved; R.N. (1945).
M.24	,,	12.10.40	U.S.N. (1945), French *Ailette* (1947); W. German *Wespe* (1963).
M.25	C. Stülcken (Hamburg)	19. 3.40	Scuttled French Atlantic port 9/44.
M.26	,,	21. 5.40	Bombed Allied aircraft Bay of Biscay 15/5/42.
M.27	,,	20.11.40	Mined Gironde Estuary 11/8/44.
M.28	,,	29. 7.40	R.N. (1945), French *Meuse* (1947); scrapped Blyth 3/5/48.
M.29	Oderwerke (Stettin)	18. 5.40	Russian *T.904* (1945).
M.30	,,	1. 6.40	Russian *T.905* (1945).
M.31	,,	13. 7.40	Torpedoed Russian MTB north of Norway 21/10/44.
M.32	,,	24. 8.40	U.S.N. (1945); scrapped Ghent 1950.
M.33	Lübecker Maschinenbau	1. 4.42	U.S.N. (1945); scrapped Ghent 1950.
M.34	,,	7. 8.42	Russian *T.906* (1945).
M.35	Schichau (Königsberg)	9.11.40	U.S.N. (1945), French *Bapaume* (1947); scrapped 1950.

NAME	BUILDER	LAUNCHED	FATE
M.36	Schichau (Königsberg)	21.12.40	Bombed Allied aircraft Great Belt 4/5/45.
M.37	Oderwerke (Stettin)	12.10.40	Torpedoed Russian MTB's. Narva Bay 4/6/44.
M.38	Atlas Werke (Bremen)	28. 2.41	R.N. (1945), French *Oise* (1945); scrapped 1955.
M.39	,,	8. 8.41	Torpedoed R.N. MTB north-west of Ouistreham 24/5/44.
M.40–80	—	—	Cancelled.
M.81	Lübecker Maschinenbau	20.12.40	U.S.N. (1945), French *Laffaux* (1947); W. German *Hummel* (1963).
M.82	,,	23. 3.41	R.N. (1945); scrapped Blyth 3/5/48.
M.83	,,	5. 6.41	Gunfire R.N. destroyers *Ashanti* and Polish *Piorun* off Cherbourg 14/6/44.
M.84	,,	3. 9.41	Scuttled Le Havre 11/8/44.
M.85	Nordseewerke (Emden)	6.12.41	R.N. (1945), French *Yser* (1947); W. German *Brummer* (1963).
M.86–100	—	—	Cancelled.
M.101	Rickmers Werft (Bremerhaven)	15. 3.41	Lost by collision west of Namsos 23/11/42.
M.102	Rickmers Werft (Bremerhaven)	1. 8.41	R.N. (1945); scrapped Blyth 24/5/48.
M.103	,,	3.12.41	Bombed Allied aircraft Ems estuary 15/6/44
M.104	,,	1. 4.42	R.N. (1945); scrapped Grays 10/5/48.
M.105–130	—	—	Cancelled.

NAME	BUILDER	LAUNCHED	FATE
M.131	Lindenau (Memel)	20.12.41	R.N. (1945); scrapped Blyth 24/5/48.
M.132	Reiherstieg (Hamburg)	7. 4.41	Torpedoed R.N. submarine off Eggeroy 20/9/44.
M.133	,,	3. 8.42	Written off as constructive total loss 14/6/44; scuttled St. Malo 1/8/44.
M.134–150	—	—	Cancelled.
M.151	Oderwerke (Stettin)	19.10.40	Russian *T.907* (1945).
M.152	,,	16.11.40	Mined off Gironde estuary 23/7/43
M.153	,,	4. 1.41	Gunfire R.N. and R.N.N. coastal forces off Ushant 10/7/43.
M.154	,,	3. 5.41	U.S.N. (1945), mercantile.
M.155	,,	19. 7.41	Russian *T.908* (1945).
M.156	,,	4.10.41	Bombed Allied aircraft L'Abervracht 6/2/44.
M.157–200	—	—	Cancelled.
M.201	Neptun Werft (Rostock)	18. 5.40	R.N. (1945); scrapped Grays, 10/5/48.
M.202	,,	29. 9.40	U.S.N. (1945), French *Craonne* (1947); scrapped 1950.
M.203	,,	29. 9.40	Russian *T.909* (1945).
M.204	,,	21.12.40	Russian *T.910* (1945).
M.205	,,	3. 5.41	U.S.N. (1945), French *Belfort* (1947), W. German *Biene* (1963).
M.206	,,	5. 5.41	Scuttled St. Malo 14/8/44.

M.207–250	—	—	Cancelled.
M.251	Deutsche Werft (Hamburg)	12. 7.40	U.S.N. (1945), French *Péronne* (1947); scrapped 1950.
M.252	,,	27. 9.40	U.S.N. (1945), French *Ancre* (1947); scrapped 1955.
M.253	,,	23.11.40	U.S.N. (1945), French *Vimy* (1947); W. German *Bremse* (1963).
M.254	,,	17. 2.41	Russian *T.911* (1945).
M.255	,,	1. 4.41	Russian *T.912* (1945).
M.256	,,	31. 5.41	Lost 5/42, salved; Russian *T.913* (1945).
M.257–260	,,	—	Cancelled.
M.261	Atlas Werke (Bremen)	10. 4.42	R.N. (1945), R.N.N. (1947), scrapped.
M.262	,,	25. 6.42	Scuttled Bordeaux 25/8/44.
M.263	,,	17.12.42	Gunfire R.N. surface forces north of Ile d'Yeu 6/8/44.
M.264	,,	19. 5.43	Bombed Allied aircraft west of Heligoland 18/7/44.
M.265	,,	21. 9.43	Russian *T.914* (1945).
M.266	,,	18. 3.44	Bombed 8th U.S.A.A.F. aircraft Kiel F.26/8/44, salved; bombed U.S.A.A. aircraft Kiel 11/3/45.
M.267	,,	13. 6.44	Russian *T.915* (1945).
M.268–270	,,	—	Cancelled.
M.271	Rickmers Werft (Bremerhaven)	42	Bombed Pauillac 5/8/44.
M.272	,,	42	R.N. (1945), R.N.N. (1947).

Minesweeper M.401, *the fo'c'sle 4·1-inch gun has been replaced by light A.A. weapons*

[*Drüppel*

TS.4 (ex-*minesweeper* M.278) *with two single T.T. on the fo'c'sle and crane aft for recovering torpedoes, about* 16 *of which could be stowed on deck*

[*Drüppel*

Minesweeper type 1940: M.261–501

The war need of the German Navy to conserve stocks of oil fuel resulted in these vessels reverting to coal-firing. The earlier units had their forward 4.1-inch gun replaced by light A.A. guns, and the later units were so completed. The final armament in the greater majority finally comprised a single 37mm. a single 20mm. A.A. guns before the bridge; two single 20mm. A.A. guns in the bridge wings; a single 20mm. A.A. gun abaft the funnel; a quadruple 20mm. A.A. mounting at the after end of the superstructure; and the 4.1-inch A.A. gun on the quarterdeck. Fifteen vessels of this series were fitted with two single torpedo tubes on the fo'c'sle for training purposes, but these were not permanently shipped and were carried, or not, as required.

Displacement: 637 tons (775 tons full).
Dimensions: 189(pp) 204½(oa) × 28 × 7/9½ feet.
Machinery: Two Marine boilers (pressure 232 lb.); two shafts; reciprocating (VTE) with Bauer-Wach exhaust turbine, S.H.P. 2,400 = $16\frac{3}{4}$ knots.
Bunkers & Coal 162 tons; 4,000 miles at 10 knots.
Radius
Armament: Two except *TS boats* one 4.1-inch A.A. (1/2 × 1), six 20mm. A.A. (1 × 4 and 2 × 1) guns; two 21-inch (2 × 1) T.T. in *TS boats* only.
Complement: 76.

NAME	BUILDER	LAUNCHED	FATE
M.273	Rickmers Werft (Bremerhaven)	43	Gunfire R.N. surface forces off Egersund 12/1/45.
M.274	,,	43	Scuttled Schelde estuary 5/9/44.
M.275	,,	25. 5.43	R.N. (1945), French (1947); discarded 1948
M.276	,,	43	Scuttled Schelde estuary 5/9/44.
M.277	,,	43	R.N. (1945), French (1947).

NAME	BUILDER	LAUNCHED	FATE
M.278 (*ex TS.4*)	Rickmers Werft (Bremerhaven)	25. 1.44	U.S.N. (1945), German *M.202* (1951), *Seestern* (1960).
M.279 (ex *TS.9*)	,,	4. 7.44	Russian *T.916* (1947).
M.280 (ex *TS.14*)	,,	44	Scrapped incomplete 5/45.
M.281–290	,,	—	Cancelled.
M.291	Lindenau (Memel)	27. 3.43	Russian *T.917* (1947).
M.292	,,	19. 6.43	Bombed Allied aircraft Gironde estuary 21/8/44.
M.293	,,	43	Rocket fire R.A.F. aircraft (18 Sqn.) Kattegat 2/5/45.
M.294	,,	4. 3.44	U.S.N. (1945), German *M.201* (1951), *Seepferd* (1960).
M.295	,,	44	Scuttled incomplete Gdynia 1945, salved and Polish *Panna Wodna*.
M.296	,,	—	Destroyed on slip 23/3/45.
M.297 (ex *TS.15*)	,,	—	Scrapped incomplete 1945.
M.298–300	,,	—	Cancelled.
M.301	Unterweser (Bremerhaven)	9. 4.41	Rocket fire R.A.F. aircraft (18 Sqn.) Skagerak 4/5/45.
M.302	,,	26. 7.41	R.N. (1945), R.N.N. (1947).
M.303	,,	29.12.41	Torpedoed Russian MTB off Kiberg 11/10/44.
M.304	,,	30. 4.42	Scuttled Bordeaux 25/8/44.
M.305	,,	20.10.42	Foundered off Brustertort 17/1/45.
M.306	,,	19.12.42	R.N. (1945), R.N.N. (1947).

[*Drüppel*

Minesweeper M.*321 survived the war and was allocated to the Royal Navy. Like all tonnage received under war reparations she was scrapped, while some other units were transferred to Allied navies, by the British*

K

NAME	BUILDER	LAUNCHED	FATE
M.307	Unterweser (Bremerhaven)	16. 6.43	Bombed Allied aircraft north of Spiekeroog 21/7/44.
M.308–320	,,	—	Cancelled.
M.321	Oderwerke (Stettin)	29. 3.41	R.N. (1945), scrapped.
M.322	,,	31. 5.41	R.N. (1945), R.N.N. (1947); scrapped Denmark 1953.
M.323	,,	9. 8.41	R.N. (1945).
M.324	,,	20. 9.41	Russian *T.918* (1945).
M.325	,,	31.10.42	Bombed Allied aircraft Pauillac 5/8/44.
M.326	,,	30. 1.43	R.N. (1945), R.N.N. (1947).
M.327	,,	12. 6.43	R.N. (1945), scrapped.
M.328	,,	12. 6.43	U.S.N. (1947), Italian *Antilope* (1949).
M.329	Lübecker Maschinenbau	27. 5.43	Bombed U.S.A.A.F. aircraft Wilhelmshaven 30/3/45.
M.330	,,	7. 2.44	Russian *T.919* (1945).
M.331–340	,,	—	Cancelled.
M.341	Neptun Werft (Rostock)	10. 6.41	Russian *T.920* (1947).
M.342	,,	11. 6.41	Russian *T.921* (1947).
M.343	,,	6.12.41	Gunfire R.N. destroyer *Ashanti* and Polish *Piorun* off Brittany 14/6/44; scuttled St. Malo 6/8/44.
M.344	,,	13.12.41	Scuttled French Atlantic port 9/44.
M.345	,,	27. 6.42	Bombed Allied aircraft French Atlantic port 18/5/43.

NAME	BUILDER	LAUNCHED	FATE
M.346	Neptun Werft (Rostock)	27. 6.42	Torpedoed Russian submarine *S.51* Tanafjord 17/7/43.
M.347	,,	7.11.42	Torpedoed and cannon fire of R.A.F. aircraft north-west of Schiermonnikoog 25/8/44.
M.348	,,	7.11.42	Russian *T.922* (1945).
M.349–360	,,	—	Cancelled.
M.361	Schichau (Königsberg)	5. 3.41	R.N. (1945), scrapped.
M.362	,,	1. 4.41	R.N. (1945), R.N.N. (1947); scrapped Denmark 1952.
M.363	,,	31. 5.41	Scuttled Bordeaux 25/8/44.
M.364	,,	9. 8.41	R.N. (1945), R.N.N. (1947).
M.365	,,	25. 7.42	R.N. (1945), R.N.N. (1947).
M.366	,,	5. 9.42	Bombed Allied aircraft St. Nazaire 8/8/44.
M.367	,,	23.12.42	Bombed Allied aircraft St. Nazaire 8/8/44.
M.368	,,	15. 2.43	Lost by collision south of Norway 15/4/45.
M.369	,,	18. 6.43	Russian *T.923* (1947).
M.370	,,	17. 7.43	Bombed Allied aircraft off Royan 12/8/44.
M.371 (ex *TS.1*)	,,	31. 7.43	U.S.N. (1945).
M.372 (ex *TS.3*)	,,	25. 9.43	Bombed Allied aircraft off Swinemünde 12/5/44.

NAME	BUILDER	LAUNCHED	FATE
M.373 (ex *TS.5*)	Schichau (Königsberg)	30.11.43	U.S.N. (1945).
M.374 (ex *TS.6*)	,,	18.12.43	U.S.N. (1945); scrapped Ghent (1950).
M.375 (ex *TS.8*)	,,	10. 3.44	U.S.N. (1945).
M.376 (ex *TS.10*)	,,	19. 4.44	Bombed Russian aircraft off Hela 11/4/45.
M.377 (ex *TS.11*)	,,	27. 6.44	Russian *T.924* (1947)
M.378 (ex *TS.13*)	,,	44	Scrapped incomplete Rostock 4/45.
M.379	,,	—	Destroyed incomplete on slip.
M.380	,,	—	Destroyed incomplete on slip.
M.381	Elsflether Werft	15. 2.41	Torpedoed R.N. submarine *Venturer* off Christiansand 12/2/45.
M.382	,,	28. 6.41	Mined north of Molde 31/1/45
M.383	,,	22.11.41	Rocket fire of Allied aircraft north of Langeoog 13/8/44.
M.384	,,	12. 9.42	Scuttled Nantes 11/8/44.
M.385	,,	43	Gunfire R.N. cruiser *Mauritius* north of Les Sables d'Olonne 15/8/44.
M.386	,,	1. 7.43	Russian *T.925* (1945).
M.387 (ex *TS.2*)	,,	43	Scuttled Lübeck 2/5/45.
M.388 (ex *TS.7*)	,,	22. 4.44	U.S.N. (1945), German *M.203* (1951); *Seehund* (1956).
M.389 (ex *TS.12*)	,,	22. 7.44	U.S.N. (1945).
M.390–400	,,	—	Scrapped incomplete or cancelled.
M.401	Rotterdam D.D.	4. 4.42	Russian *T.926* (1945).
M.402	,,	4. 4.42	Bombed Allied aircraft Boulogne 15/6/44.

NAME	BUILDER	LAUNCHED	FATE
M.403	Rotterdam D.D.	15. 9.42	Bombed Allied aircraft south-west of Gothenburg 19/4/45.
M.404	,,	14.10.42	U.S.N. (1945), French (1945).
M.405	,,	42	Russian *T.927* (1945).
M.406	,,	30.12.42	Russian *T.928* (1945).
M.407	,,	43	Russian *T.929* (1945).
M.408	,,	43	U.S.N. (1945), French (1948).
M.409–410	,,	—	Cancelled.
M.411	De Schelde (Flushing)	22. 8.42	Russian *T.930* (1945).
M.412	,,	6. 9.42	Blown-up Granville 9/3/45 following stranding.
M.413	,,	42	Bombed Russian aircraft Narva Bay 21/7/44.
M.414	,,	9.11.42	Torpedoed Allied aircraft west of Texel 17/5/43.
M.415	,,	16. 1.43	Russian T.931 (1947).
M.416	,,	43	Gunfire of R.N. destroyer south of Norway 12/11/44.
M.417–420	,,	—	Cancelled.
M.421	(Wilton-Fijenoord (Schiedam)	29.11.41	Mined off Kolberg 13/2/45.
M.422	,,	42	Bombed R.A.F. aircraft off St. Malo 4/8/44.
M.423	,,	18.10.42	Russian *T.932* (1946).
M.424	,,	18.10.42	Bombed Allied aircraft St. Malo 5/8/44; salved 7/46 and R.N. French (1948).

NAME	BUILDER	LAUNCHED	FATE
M.425	(Wilton-Fijenoord (Schiedam)	18.10.42	Russian *T.933* (1947).
M.426	,,	18.10.42	Bombed Allied aircraft east of Skagens 12/9/44.
M.427	,,	18.10.42	Gunfire R.N. destroyer Rekkefjord 13/11/44.
M.428	,,	18.10.42	Bombed Allied aircraft St. Nazaire 8/8/44.
M.429–430	,,	—	Cancelled.
M.431	Netherlands Dock & Sbdg. (Amsterdam)	7. 3.42	Russian *T.934* (1945).
M.432	,,	7. 3.42	U.S.N. (1945), French (1945), *Suippe* (1947); discarded 1953.
M.433	,,	11. 4.42	Bombed Allied aircraft Vegafjord 27/10/44.
M.434	,,	11. 4.42	U.S.N. (1945), French (1945).
M.435	,,	27. 6.42	Bombed Allied aircraft north of Ameland 14/5/44.
M.436	,,	27. 6.42	R.N. (1945), R.N.N. (1947).
M.437	,,	27. 6.42	Russian *T.935* (1945).
M.438	,,	27. 6.42	Bombed Allied aircraft St. Nazaire 8/8/44.
M.439–440	,,	—	Cancelled.
M.441	P. Smit (Rotterdam)	19. 6.42	U.S.N. (1945) German *M.205* (1952), *Seelöwe* (1956).

NAME	BUILDER	LAUNCHED	FATE
M.442	P. Smit (Rotterdam)	42	U S.N. (1945), French *Marne* (1947); scrapped 1953.
M.443	,,	15. 9.42	Russian *T.936* (1946).
M.444	,,	30.11.42	Bombed Allied aircraft and mined off Brest 14/8/44.
M.445	,,	12.12.42	Bombed U.S.A.A.F. aircraft Hamburg 31/12/44.
M.446	,,	3. 2.43	Russian *T.937* (1947).
M.447–450	,,	—	Cancelled.
M.451	Gusto Werft (Schiedam)	24.12.41	Wrecked off Helsinki 31/1/44.
M.452	,,	19.12.42	U.S.N. (1945), French (1945), *Aisne* (1947); scrapped 1949.
M.453	,,	15.12.42	U.S.N. (1945); scrapped Ghent 1949.
M.454	,,	43	U.S.N. (1945), French (1945).
M.455	,,	7.12.42	Bombed Allied aircraft Cuxhaven 4/45, salved.
M.456	,,	3. 3.43	Russian *T.938* (1947).
M.457–458	,,	—	Cancelled.
M.459	Netherlands Dock & Sbdg. (Amsterdam)	42	Bombed Russian aircraft Narva Bay 10/4/44.
M.460	,,	31. 7.42	U.S.N. (1945), German *M.204* (1951), *Seeigel* (1956).
M.461	,,	24.10.42	Russian *T.939* (1945).
M.462	,,	27. 1.43	Bombed Allied aircraft north of Skagens 12/9/44.

[*Drüppel*

Minesweeper M.608, *initially allocated to the United States Navy, was later converted into a passenger ferry*

NAME	BUILDER	LAUNCHED	FATE
M.463	Netherlands Dock & Sbdg. (Amsterdam)	43	Scuttled Bordeaux 25/8/44.
M.464-466	,,	—	Cancelled.

NAME	BUILDER	LAUNCHED	FATE
M.467	Van der Giessen (Krimpen)	9. 1.42	Russian *T.940* (1945).
M.468	,,	9. 7.42	Torpedoed Russian MTB west of Namsos 12/8/44.
M.469	,,	9. 7.42	Torpedoed R.N. MTB north-west of Vlieland 4/7/44.
M.470	,,	21.10.42	Russian *T.941* (1947).
M.471	,,	21.10.42	Bombed Allied aircraft Den Helder 25/9/44.
M.472–474	,,	—	Cancelled.
M.475	J. & K. Smit (Kinderdijk)	29. 8.42	U.S.N. (1945), French (1945).
M.476	,,	3.10.42	U.S.N. (1945), French (1947).
M.477–482	,,	—	Cancelled.
M.483	Boele's (Slikkerveer)	16. 5.42	Mined English Channel 15/6/43.
M.484	,,	25. 8.42	Russian *T.942* (1945).
M.485	,,	—	Cancelled.
M.486	Verschure (Amsterdam)	42	Gunfire R.N. cruiser *Bellona*, destroyers *Ashanti* and *Tartar* and R.C.N. *Haida* and *Huron* off Ile d'Yeu 6/8/44.
M.487–488	,,	—	Cancelled.
M.489	L. Smit (Kinderdijk)	28. 8.42	Torpedoed R.N. M.T.B. off Mosterhavn 23/12/44.
M 490–494	,,	—	Cancelled.

NAME	BUILDER	LAUNCHED	FATE
M.495	Gebr. Pot (Bolnes)	4. 9.42	U.S.N. (1945), French (1947).
M.496	,,	12. 1.43	Russian *T.943* (1947).
M.497–501	,,	—	Cancelled.
M.601	Neptun Werft (Rostock)	31. 8.44	R.N. (1945); scrapped Middlesbrough 20/4/48.
M.602	,,	21.10.44	R.N. (1945).
M.603	,,	2.11.44	R.N. (1945).
M.604	,,	10.11.44	R.N. (1945); scrapped Tyne 28/3/48.
M.605	,,	13.12.44	R.N. (1945).
M.606	,,	20.12.44	U.S.N. (1945); scrapped Ghent 1950.
M.607	,,	30.12.44	U.S.N. (1945), mercantile *Hörhum* (1948), *Christian Ivers* (1960), *Hanne Scarlet* (1953), *Salvatore Lauro* (1962).
M.608	,,	20. 1.45	U.S.N. (1945), mercantile *Amrum* (1948), *Harald Ivers* (1950), *Lili Scarlet* (1953), *Elena P.* (1964).
M.609	,,	29. 1.45	U.S.N. (1945); scrapped Dunston 17/2/48.
M.610	,,	27. 2.45	U.S.N. (1945); scrapped Ghent 1950.
M.611	,,	12. 3.45	U.S.N. (1945), mercantile *Wangerooge* (1958), German *M.206* (1952), *Seeschlange* (1956).
M.612	,,	23. 3.45	R.N. (1945).

Minesweeper M.612

[*Drüppel*

Minesweeper type 1943: M.601–886, 1001–1050

These vessels were, in addition to minesweeping, designed to act as escort or torpedo recovery vessels. For the former role the forward 4.1-inch gun was re-introduced and the hull lengthened some 20 feet to accommodate it. They could be equipped for minelaying and stow twenty-four mines for this purpose.

Displacement: 668 tons (821 tons full).
Dimensions: 207(pp) 224(oa) × 29½ × 6½/8½ feet.
Machinery: Two Marine boilers (pressure 232 lb.); two shafts; reciprocating (VTE) with Bauer-Wach exhaust turbine, I.H.P. 2,400 = 16½ knots.
Bunkers & Radius Coal 136 tons; 3,600 miles at 10 knots.
Armament: Two 4.1-inch A.A. (2 × 1), two 37mm. A.A. (2 × 1), eight 20mm. A.A. (1 × 4 and 4 × 1) guns.
Complement: 107.

NAME	BUILDER	LAUNCHED	FATE
M.613–616	Neptun Werft (Rostock)	45	Scrapped incomplete Rostock 1945.
M.617–633	,,	—	Scrapped on slip.
M.634–666	,,	—	Cancelled.
M.667–800	,,	—	Cancelled.
M.801	Schichau (Königsberg)	9. 9.44	U.S.N. (1945), Italian *Gazzella* (ex-*B.3*—1949).
M.802	,,	29. 9.44	Bombed U.S.A.A.F. aircraft Kiel 3/4/45.
M.803	,,	19.10.44	U.S.N. (1945), Italian *Diano* (ex-*B.2*—1949).
M.804	,,	1.11.44	Bombed U.S.A.A.F. aircraft Kiel 11/3/45.
M.805	,,	9.11.44	Bombed U.S.A.A.F. aircraft Kiel 11/3/45.
M.806	,,	21.11.44	R.N. (1945); scrapped Tyne 28/3/48.
M.807	,,	13. 1.45	Towed incomplete to Rostock 1/45.
M.808	,,	45	Towed incomplete to Rostock 1/45.
M.809–813	,,	—	Scrapped incomplete.
M.814–816	,,	—	Scrapped on slip.
M.817–1000	,,	—	Cancelled.
M.1001–1050	Korneuburg Werft (Vienna)	—	Cancelled.

Minesweeper M.806, *like the remainder of her class, was of prefabricated construction, the hull being divided into six main sections—plus the bridge and superstructure—which were assembled at three main shipyards*

Ex-R.Neth.N. minesweepers: M.551–553

460 tons (585 tons full): 183(wl) 186(oa) $\times$ 25½ $\times$ 6½/7¼ feet: two Yarrow boilers (pressure ... lb.), two-shaft reciprocating (VTE) I.H.P. 1,600 = 15½ knots, O.F. 110 tons (2,350 miles at 11 knots): one 3-inch A.A., four 20mm. A.A. (1 $\times$ 2 and 2 $\times$ 1) guns, fitted for minelaying: complement 59.

NAME	BUILDER	LAUNCHED	FATE
M.551 (ex-*Peter Florisz*)	P. Smit (Rotterdam)	11.5.37	Scuttled Enkhuizen 14/5/40, salved and German; retroceded 1945.
M.552 (ex-*Abraham van der Hulst*)	Werft Gusto (Schiedam)	31.5.37	Scuttled Ijsselmeer 14/5/40, salved and German; retroceded 1945.
M.553 (ex-*Willem van Ewijk (ii)*)	P. Smit (Rotterdam)	18.4.40	Mined Baltic 21/4/44; salved 20/7/44, retroceded 1945 and scrapped.

Ex-R.D.N. minesweepers: MA.1–6

274 tons (305 tons full): 169(pp) 176½(oa) $\times$ 20¾ $\times$ 6½/7¼ feet: one Thornycroft boiler (pressure ... lb.), one-shaft .... geared turbines S.H.P. 2,200 = 19 knots, O.F. 30 tons (.,... miles at .. knots): two 3-inch (2 $\times$ 1), four 20mm. A.A. (4 $\times$ 1), four 8mm. A.A. (2 $\times$ 2) guns, fitted for minelaying: complement 47.

MA.1 (ex-*Söløven*)	Naval Dockyard (Copenhagen)	3.12.38	Scuttled Korsor 29/8/43, salved and German, *Vs.61* (1944); retroceded 1945.
MA.2 (ex-*Söbjörnen*)	,,	16.2.39	Scuttled Copenhagen 29/8/43, salved and German; scrapped 1945.

NAME	BUILDER	LAUNCHED	FATE
MA.3 (ex-*Söulven*)	Naval Dockyard (Copenhagen)	1939	Scuttled Copenhagen 29/8/43, salved and German; scrapped 1945.
MA.4 (ex-*Söridderen*)	,,	11.4.42	Scuttled Korsor 29/8/43, salved and German, *Vs.62* (1944); retroceded 1945.
MA.5 (ex-*Söhesten*)	,,	30.4.42	Scuttled Kalundborg 29/8/43, salved and German, *Vs.63* (1944); retroceded 1945.
MA.6 (ex-*Söhunden*)	,,	16.5.42	Scuttled Kogebucht 29/8/43, salved and German, *Vs.64* (1945); retroceded 1945.

Seaplane tender: WALTER HOLZAPFEL

1,400 tons (1,586 tons full): 249¼(pp) 259¼(oa) × 38 × 9¾/11½ feet: two-shafts, Sulzer diesel motors, B.H.P. 7,600 = 19½ knots, O.F. 75 tons (1,500 miles at 15 knots): two 37mm. A.A. (2 ×1), four 20mm. A.A. (1 × 4) guns, four 21-inch (1 × 4) T.T.: complement 84.

NAME	BUILDER	LAUNCHED	FATE
Walter Holzapfel	Norderwerft (Hamburg)	1939	R.N. *Deepwater* (1946)

INDEX

(Vol. 1=I, Vol,2=II)